Routine Blood Results Explained

Dr Andrew Blann
PhD FRCPath

Consultant Clinical Scientist
and Honorary Senior Lecturer in Medicine

Haemostasis, Thrombosis and Vascular Biology Unit
University Department of Medicine
City Hospital, Birmingham, UK

Routine Blood Results Explained

Dr Andrew Blann

ISBN: 9781905539-88-8

First published 2006
Second edition 2007
Third revised edition 2013

British Library Cataloguing in Publication Data

A catalogue record for this book is available from the British Library

Notice

Clinical practice and medical knowledge constantly evolve. Standard safety precautions must be followed, but, as knowledge is broadened by research, changes in practice, treatment and drug therapy may become necessary or appropriate. Readers must check the most current product information provided by the manufacturer of each drug to be administered and verify the dosages and correct administration, as well as contraindications. It is the responsibility of the practitioner, utilising the experience and knowledge of the patient, to determine dosages and the best treatment for each individual patient. Any brands mentioned in this book are as examples only and are not endorsed by the publisher. Neither the publisher nor the authors assume any liability for any injury and/or damage to persons or property arising from this publication.

To contact M&K Publishing write to:

M&K Update Ltd · The Old Bakery · St. John's Street

Keswick · Cumbria CA12 5AS

Tel: 01768 773030 · Fax: 01768 781099

publishing@mkupdate.co.uk

www.mkupdate.co.uk

Designed and typeset by Mary Blood

Printed in England by H&H Reeds, Penrith

Contents

Part 4: Appendices

Prefaces

Preface to the first edition

The objective of this slim volume is to provide help in understanding and interpreting the majority of the normal blood results found in most NHS hospitals. The text, based on the routine blood report forms sent out from Pathology Departments, has evolved from lecture notes given to various healthcare professionals (nurses, phlebotomists, pharmacists, radiographers and physiotherapists, etc.) attending day-long courses on exactly these topics.

An additional objective is to keep the material simple and focused. Thus, the reader seeking a comprehensive in-depth explanation of a wide number of tests and their exact relationship to various clinical diseases will be disappointed. However, it is impossible to fully understand pathology without a sure grounding in physiology. Hence there will be an adequate and clear explanation of those aspects of the body that are necessary to understand a particular test and its associated problems. Examples are provided that will illustrate particular points; it must be stressed that these are not exact and perfect case reports, merely aids in understanding the concepts developed in the text.

Focusing on 'routine' blood tests therefore, by definition, excludes tests less frequently reported. In this volume, tests that will be absent from the general discussion are, for example, platelet volume, red cell mass, magnesium, and reproductive hormones. These omissions are not indicative of lack of importance, merely lack of regular requesting. The emphasis is also on the adult, so paediatric tests (by and large) will not be mentioned.

Preface to the second edition

With such a brief interval between the first and second editions, there are few major changes in the practice of routine blood science worthy of addressing – most changes to the text are merely the correction of typographical errors present in the first edition. However, the second edition has benefited from some structural changes, notably the merging of separate chapters on calcium and the thyroid into a single section. New text, generally in response to comments from readers and delegates on M&K courses, includes more details on blood transfusion, and also a completely new chapter with sections on pregnancy, paediatrics, and on immunology as applied to the inflammatory auto-immune connective tissue diseases such as rheumatoid arthritis.

In 2007 haematology is involved in a transition in reporting haemoglobin results from grams per decilitre (e.g. 13.5g/dL) to grams per litre, which therefore becomes 135g/L.

Therefore it is simply a question of moving the decimal point one place to the right. Indeed, many hospitals have already made this transition. However, in the present setting I will retain the historical units.

Preface to the third edition

The six-year interval since the second edition has seen many changes. There have been changes in units, such as the transformation of haemoglobin measurements from g/dL to g/L, but also the merging of haematology with biochemistry, blood transformation and immunology to form blood science. Accordingly, in this edition, there are more details of immunology, immunological diseases, and the blood tests involved.

A parallel series of changes has seen the growing responsibility of nurses, podiatrists and physiotherapists. Many are now taking on new roles such as, in sequence:

- Examining the patient
- Proposing a diagnosis
- Venesecting (taking blood)
- Ordering blood tests
- Interpreting the results
- Managing the condition

Previously, these roles were undertaken by medical staff only, but it is now clear that appropriately trained professionals can be equipped to carry out these tasks.

The objective of this book is to support and enable these professionals to be successful in their new roles. To this end, wherever possible, each chapter will conclude with a brief case study. More complete case reports, reflecting the different aspects of primary and secondary care, are presented in the concluding chapters.

Introduction

'…it is estimated that the data received by clinicians from Medical Laboratories constitutes 70–80% of the information they rely on to make major medical decisions…'

The Biomedical Scientist 2005, **49**: 38.

This statement is effectively why blood tests are important – they provide three times as much information as do all other sources (history, examination, symptoms, imaging, etc.) combined. Fortunately, the vast majority of routine blood tests (certainly in routine, emergency and critical care medicine) fall easily into one of two groups: haematology (with blood transfusion) and biochemistry. The most recently developed discipline, immunology, now deserves a chapter of its own. The layout of the volume will therefore follow this pattern. Each of the two major sections breaks down into individual chapters and concludes with a dedicated example.

Knowledge is nothing without practice. Therefore the book will conclude with case studies designed to help the practitioner. These cases will look at both primary and secondary care.

What is done where?

In some Pathology Departments, certain tests are done in the Haematology Laboratory, whilst in other hospitals the same test may be performed in the Biochemistry Laboratory. Examples of this include iron studies, C-reactive protein (CRP), and testing for vitamin B_{12} and serum folate. However, these tests are done on serum obtained from whole blood that has not been anticoagulated. The reader is referred to their own Pathology Service for the correct tube for the test and the destination of these requests.

Overall, our colleagues in the Pathology Department, regardless of discipline, would far rather set the position clear in a phone call than go through the bother of phoning back that a fresh sample in the correct tube must be obtained.

If in doubt – PHONE! !

A note on units

In the real world, of course, results are almost unanimously described as the numbers themselves (e.g. a haemoglobin of 125 or a cholesterol of 5) instead of the more correct way where the result is described with its unit (i.e. 125g/L and 8mmol/L). This shorthand is (almost) universally accepted, and generally makes life considerably easier. It matters not so much that the correct unit of the average size of a red blood cell is described fully (for example, as 112fL, or in shorthand simply as 112) but it does matter that the particular cell is much larger than can be expected in complete health, and therefore implies ill-health.

Reference ranges

In trying to define ill-health, we generally use good health as a comparator. Thus a healthy person can be expected to have a certain healthy blood result profile. However, these values are sometimes not well established and are subject to change. Furthermore, there are many normal (healthy) people whose blood result may not be in the expected range of values – but this does not necessarily mean they are ill. From this point of view, the 'normal' values could more accurately be called the 'desirable' values and the 'reference' range could reasonably be termed a 'target' range. Nevertheless, for the purposes of this volume, the reference range will be cited. Haematology and biochemistry are very quantitative sciences, immunology less so. Consequently, the reference range is important. The precise definition of the reference range in use at a particular hospital is crucial and is not transferable to another hospital. This may be because of small differences in the technical manner in which tests are carried out. Furthermore, reference ranges may well (and certainly should) reflect the local population served by the hospital. This is important as different catchment populations may vary considerably, especially in ethnicity.

It is also becoming the case that results will be provided with a reference range that suits the particular patient (for example, a male reference range for blood from a man, a paediatric reference range for an infant, etc.). Care must therefore be taken when comparing samples and reference ranges. In the future, an age-specific and race-specific reference range may also be produced.

As mentioned in the preface to this edition, haematology and biochemistry are rapidly merging and evolving into blood science, in which the numbers definitely mean something. Many practitioners will seek guidance from, and will base treatment on, these blood results. One of the first questions to ask is therefore 'is the result acceptable?' In many cases, this boils down to whether or not the results match the reference range, which is presumably derived from normal (i.e. healthy) individuals. However, merely having a result that is a fraction outside the reference range does not necessarily imply a serious pathology. Conversely, a result that is very far from the reference range carries with it an implication of a problem, but several tests (as well as clinical signs, history, etc.) are still needed to be sure of a particular diagnosis.

Abbreviations

ALL	Acute lymphoblastic leukaemia
AML	Acute myeloid leukaemia
ANA	Antinuclear antibodies
APTT	Activated partial thromboplastin time
ARF	Acute renal failure
CK	Creatine kinase
CLL	Chronic lymphocytic leukaemia
CML	Chronic myeloid leukaemia
COPD	Chronic obstructive pulmonary disease
CRF	Chronic renal failure
CRP	C-reactive protein
DKA	Diabetic ketoacidosis
DVT	Deep vein thrombosis
ECG	Electrocardiogram
EDTA	Ethylenediamine tetra-aceticacid
ESR	Erythrocyte sedimentation rate
FBC	Full blood count
GFR	Glomerular filtration rate
Hct	Haematocrit
Hb	Haemoglobin
HbA1c	Glycated haemoglobin
HDL-cholesterol	High density lipoprotein cholesterol
INR	International normalised ratio
LDL-cholesterol	Low density lipoprotein cholesterol

LFT	Liver function test
LMWH	Low molecular weight heparin
MCH	Mean cell haemoglobin
MCHC	Mean cell haemoglobin concentration
MCV	Mean cell volume
OGTT	Oral glucose tolerance test
PTH	Parathyroid hormone
PSA	Prostate specific antigen
PT	Prothrombin time
PTT	Partial thromboplastin time
PE	Pulmonary embolus
RBCC/RCC	Red blood cell count/red cell count
RhF	Rheumatoid factor
T4	Thyroxine
TSH	Thyroid stimulating hormone
U&Es	Urea and electrolytes
VTE	Venous thromboembolism
WBCC/WCC	White blood cell count/white cell count

Part 1

Haematology, Blood Transfusion and Immunology

Objectives and scope

The learning objectives for Part 1 are overleaf. The purpose of the Haematology Laboratory is to provide assistance in diagnosing, monitoring and treating patients. The Blood Transfusion Laboratory provides blood components (mostly red cells, but also coagulation factors and the blood protein albumin) for patients at risk of potentially life-threatening situations. The Immunology Laboratory is generally concerned with antibodies, often reacting with the patient's own tissues, and so causing autoimmunity.

In order to provide clinical practitioners with the information they need, the components of the blood are analysed, almost always in custom-designed equipment. Of course, all blood tubes and forms must be fully labelled by those taking the blood in order to minimise the risk of (possibly fatal) error. Indeed, the laboratory will be well within its rights to decline to test a sample that is incorrectly or inadequately labelled.

There are three basic blood tubes that are used in these disciplines. A full blood count (FBC) is performed on blood that is anticoagulated with ethylenediamine tetra-acetic acid (EDTA). Coagulation tests are invariably done on plasma that is obtained from whole blood anticoagulated with sodium citrate. The erythrocyte sedimentation rate (ESR) may be assessed on blood that is held within its own dedicated glass tube: blood clotting in this tube is also prevented by sodium citrate. However, in some cases, the ESR can be measured using the same sample as is the FBC. For blood transfusion, an EDTA or a tube free of an anticoagulant (providing serum) is often used. Immunologists can work with serum or plasma, but for cell work the blood must be anticoagulated. Once more, if you are in even the slightest doubt about which vacutainer to take for whichever test – PHONE!!

Testing can only be performed on blood that is collected in the correct tube. Failure to do so will, at best, result in a polite phone call from the lab explaining the problem and its remedy. At worst, a report will be returned a day or so later with a comment such as 'inappropriate blood sample received, please repeat'. To help this, many blood tubes have different-coloured tops to make this process easier and minimise errors.

Fortunately, haematology can be divided very easily into three different areas. These are the red blood cell, the white blood cell and coagulation. The most important aspects of each of these are, in turn, anaemia, infection and neoplasia, and thrombosis and haemorrhage. (Blood transfusion and immunology are addressed in their own chapters, where a transfusion reaction and autoantibodies, respectively, are key.)

Finally, it would be good if the reader could translate these concepts into 'real-life' interpretation, such as the implications of a haemoglobin count of 84g/L, with or without a white blood cell count of 15×10^9/L, the possible problems and benefits of INR of 4.0, the consequences of an incompatible blood transfusion, and a knowledge of autoimmunity, hypersensitivity and immunodeficiency.

Learning objectives –
Haematology, blood transfusion and immunology

Having completed this section, the reader will:

1. **Appreciate the importance of different anticoagulants and glass tubes for the different blood tests requested.**
   These are EDTA (for a full blood count) and sodium citrate (for coagulation) ESR may require its own special tube. The Blood Bank generally needs a sample of clotted blood or blood taken into EDTA.

2. **Recognise the major areas of interest:**
   - The red blood cell
   - The white blood cell
   - Coagulation
   - Blood transfusion
   - Immunology

3. **Describe major problems associated with each of these areas, e.g., respectively:**
   - Anaemia
   - Infection/neoplasia
   - Thrombosis/haemorrhage
   - An incompatible blood transfusion
   - Autoantibodies

4. **Interpret simple haematological results such as:**
   - A haemoglobin of 8.4g/L
   - A white cell count of 15×109/L
   - A prothrombin time of 25 seconds.
   - A high titre of antinuclear antibodies

5. **Understand the importance of the Haematology Laboratory**

The haematology 'syllabus'

The form shown in Figure 1 is the full blood count (FBC). This is the most requested haematology test, and this example was produced by the author's laboratory for the end user (i.e. the requesting practitioner). This form will generally end up in the patient's notes. Apart from the usual demographic details (age, sex, hospital number, ward, consultant, etc.), the report offers (from left to right) a column of abbreviations (particular tests), a column of numbers (the result), another column of numbers and letters (units), and finally a column of numbers (the [male] normal or target range).

The FBC has details of red blood cells, white blood cells and platelets. The main objective of this section of the book is to explain to you what all of this means.

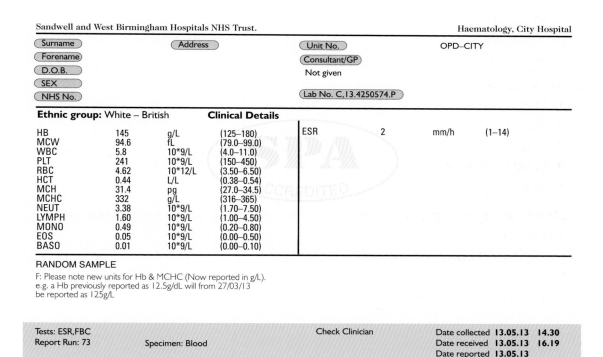

Figure 1: Haematology Report Form

The red blood cell

Key words:

Haemoglobin (Hb)

Red blood cell count (RBCC)

Haematocrit (Hct)

Red cell indices:

    Mean cell volume (MCV)

    Mean cell haemoglobin (MCH)

    Mean cell haemoglobin concentration (MCHC)

Erythrocyte sedimentation rate (ESR)

Plasma viscosity (NB: not strictly to do with the red blood cell)

Key pathological expressions:

Anaemia

Polycythaemia

Thalassaemia

Sickle cell disease

An explanation of terms:

Haemoglobin (Hb)

Haemoglobin is undoubtedly the index most frequently referred to in clinical haematology. It is a protein designed to carry oxygen from the lungs to the tissues, where the oxygen is given up to participate in respiration, the process by which energy is obtained.

    The reference range varies between the sexes. Lower levels in menstruating women seem obvious, but in post-menopausal women levels are still lower than in age-matched men, as the latter produce testosterone to stimulate red cell production. We know this because men who have lost their testes to accident or disease see their haemoglobin levels fall.

Red blood cell count (RBCC)

Red blood cells carry haemoglobin in the blood. Red blood cells are unusual as they lack a nucleus, thus providing additional flexibility to penetrate the smallest capillaries and so deliver oxygen to distant cells and tissues. They are the most abundant cell in the blood (often called erythrocytes), and numbers can also vary between the sexes for the same reason as haemoglobin.

Haematocrit (Hct)

The haematocrit index expresses that proportion, as a percentage (as above), or decimal (say 0.43) of whole blood, that is taken up by all the blood cells. Since there are approximately 1000 more red blood cells per unit volume than white blood cells, and 20 times as many (tiny) platelets, the red cells make up the major proportion of the haematocrit. Consequently, at the practical level, this index indicates the proportion of red blood cells that makes up the whole blood pool. The haematocrit also varies with age.

Red blood cell indices

The red blood cell indices are:

- Mean cell volume (MCV), which is the size of the average (mean) red blood cell. Note the stress is on 'average', as each index is the mean of millions of individual cells.
- Mean cell haemoglobin (MCH), which as the name implies, simply reports the average amount (mass) of haemoglobin in the cell. It does not take into account the size of the cell.
- Mean cell haemoglobin concentration (MCHC), which is the average concentration of haemoglobin inside the average size cell.

Error may easily be introduced. For example, an MCV of, shall we say, 90fL, may arise from cells with very diverse size, ranging from 70 to 110. Cells of such varying size must imply one or more pathological processes (such as alcoholism). But the same MCV of 90 may also be the sum of a very well-regulated population of cells that vary from, in this example, 87 to 93. For this reason, MCV is probably the most useful of the three indices, especially when investigating different types of anaemia, as we shall see.

Because several of the red cell values are mathematically derived from some of the others, it is entirely possible for any one of them to be outside the normal range whilst the other five are apparently normal. Thus one must consider all six red cell indices (and possibly some others) together to obtain a full picture. In the author's laboratory, the haematology analyser provides the Hb, RBCC and MCV results directly from the blood provided, then (simply speaking) calculates the Hct from the RBCC times the MCV, the MCH by the Hb divided by the RBCC, and the MCHC by the Hb divided by the Hct, with adjustments (e.g. multiply or divide by 10 or 100).

Erythrocyte sedimentation rate (ESR)

The ESR is also a global score of physical aspects of the blood, and is simple to understand. The result is obtained by allowing a thin column of blood to settle down under the influence of gravity. As it does so, the red blood cells will separate from the plasma, so that after an hour, a band of clear plasma will sit atop the red blood cells. The fall in the level of the red blood cells is then recorded as mm/hour. The effects of platelets and white blood cells are minimal and are ignored. It is therefore unique in requiring no sophisticated machinery and few technical skills.

An increased ESR can be caused by many factors, including cancer, infections, anaemia, inflammation, renal failure, rheumatoid arthritis, multiple myeloma and tuberculosis. It is increased soon after myocardial infarction, and is also heavily influenced by plasma proteins.

Some laboratories have a more liberal normal range, e.g. <20mm/hour, especially in the elderly.

Plasma viscosity

Plasma viscosity does not really have much to do with red blood cells, but is in this chapter purely for convenience. This index provides an idea of how thick or thin the plasma has become – whether it is thinner, and more like water (tending towards a low result of less than 1.5), or thicker and more like treacle (tending towards a high result, over 1.72).

Viscosity records a global property of the plasma, not individual molecules. Indeed, the molecules that make up the major component of viscosity include fibrinogen, albumin and some proteins involved in clotting. There is also a relationship between plasma viscosity and total plasma protein concentration, and often with the haematocrit and the amount of water in the blood.

What are red cells for?

The answer to this question is easy: to carry oxygen. This gas is required in the process of respiration, where energy is obtained from molecules such as glucose and certain fatty acids. Muscles require oxygen for the energy needed to contract. If this oxygen is insufficient, there may be pain. In the case of muscles of the intestines, this may manifest as abdominal discomfort and cramps. If muscles of the rib cage and diaphragm fail to get enough oxygen, this may lead to problems with breathing and shortness of breath. Insufficient oxygen to the brain may lead to forgetfulness, personality changes and what may seem to be early Alzheimer's disease. General symptoms include tiredness and lethargy.

These symptoms of insufficient oxygen (hypoxia) may be due to any combination of pathologies. Oxygen in the inhaled air must first cross the alveoli and enter the pulmonary circulation, a process that will be impaired by lung disease such as COPD, emphysema and pneumonia. But even well-oxygenated blood may not be delivered to the body if the heart is functioning poorly, perhaps because of valve disease, cardiomyopathy, heart failure (with an inadequate ejection fraction), left ventricular aneurysm, and the consequences of myocardial infarction. Blood passage around the body may be impaired by atherosclerosis, and in the tissues the movement of oxygen to the cells may be impaired by oedema and cellulitis.

However, if lung function is good, the heart is working well and there is no barrier to blood or oxygen moving into the cells, and the patient still complains of tiredness, lethargy, and shortness of breath, then only one major pathology remains – anaemia.

Anaemia

The oxygen-carrying capacity of the blood is a function not only of the amount of haemoglobin in each cell, but also the number of red blood cells and, to a lesser extent, the haematocrit. Thus, someone with a low MCH but a high RBCC may well have the same oxygen-carrying capacity as another person with a higher MCH but a lower RBCC. Red cells can also contribute to clotting.

Haemoglobin, RBCC, Hct and the three red cell indices of MCV, MCH and MCHC are requested in order to assess the individual's oxygen-carrying capacity. When an individual is having difficulty performing their most basic physiological and lifestyle demands, they could be anaemic. Some authorities will define anaemia as a level of haemoglobin below a certain level. However, a haemoglobin level of, say, 115g/L may well be perfectly adequate for an elderly person with few physiological requirements and a relatively quiet life. Conversely, the same haemoglobin level in a younger person with a very active lifestyle, perhaps including sports, will be inadequate. Thus the medical state of the individual as a whole person should be considered, not merely an arbitrary number at which one acts. An alternative view of anaemia may be the level at which concern arises, and at which further investigations are considered. Certainly, anaemia should not be seen merely as that level that automatically requires a blood transfusion, a therapy that many consider should be reserved only for life-saving situations (see Chapter 4).

This brings us to an important equation:

$$\textbf{Abnormal results x symptoms = disease}$$

This formula means that if someone has a low haemoglobin (perhaps 115, as in the above example) but is asymptomatic, then they don't have a disease (in this case, anaemia). Conversely, if the patient is tired, lethargic, pale and short of breath (see Table 1 below), with a haemoglobin of 140, they can't possibly be anaemic. Therefore their symptoms must be due to some other pathology, or maybe several pathologies. However, if your patient does indeed exhibit all these symptoms, and also has a low haemoglobin, then they *are* anaemic, and so warrant further investigation and possibly restorative treatment.

More serious signs of anaemia include jaundice, splenomegaly, hepatomegaly, angina, cardiac failure and fever, although these may of course arise from other conditions. To be sure of the diagnosis, we need more information about the type of anaemia, and how it came about.

Table 1: Signs and symptoms of anaemia

Signs:
- Pallor (especially of the conjunctiva)
- Tachycardia (pulse rate over 100 beats per minute)
- Glossitis (swollen and painful tongue)
- Koilonychia (spoon nails
- Dark urine (a sign of red cell destruction)

Symptoms:
- Decreased work and/or exercise capacity
- Fatigue, lethargy, 'tired all the time'
- Weakness
- Dizziness
- Palpitations
- Shortness of breath (especially on exertion)
- Rarely: headaches, tinnitus, taste disturbance

The aetiology and classification of anaemia

Anaemia may be classified in many ways (see Table 2, page 13).

Since red blood cells are produced in the bone marrow, infiltration of this tissue by cancer or other cells will inevitably lead to reduced production of red cells, and thus anaemia. Anaemia is also a fundamental aspect of aplastic anaemia, where the other functions of the bone marrow (i.e. the production of platelets and normal white blood cells) are also depressed. As we shall see, this is also the case in leukaemia, where many abnormal white blood cells make up the tumour. Our present medical approach offers various drugs in an attempt to solve many problems. However, few, if any, drugs are free of undesirable side effects, and one of these side effects can be bone marrow suppression. Thus many drugs will require frequent monitoring to check for the development of, for example, low levels of red blood cells.

Poor nutrition will also result in anaemia, such as a diet lacking essential nutrients like iron, vitamin B_{12} or folate. However, the diet itself may be adequate, but other factors may cause anaemia, such as failure to produce special proteins to aid the passage of the minerals and vitamins across the gut wall and into the blood (i.e. malabsorption).

Problems with other organs may also contribute to anaemia. Chronic liver disease may be a factor, as the liver produces molecules that store, and others that transport, essential iron and vitamins around the body (such as the specialised protein transferrin for carrying iron). Likewise, intestinal disease or malabsorption may lead to anaemia, as the ability to absorb essential minerals and vitamins will be impaired. The kidney produces a hormone, erythropoietin, to stimulate the bone marrow to produce red blood cells. Thus chronic renal failure may also contribute to anaemia.

Haemolytic anaemia is the bursting, destruction, or inappropriate break-up of red blood cells. Possible mechanisms for this include physical destruction by, for example, a poorly functioning mechanical heart valve, prolonged heavy exercise, or long marches undertaken by members of the armed forces. Certain individuals are sensitive to drugs (such as antibiotics) that stick onto the surface of red blood cells and render them more susceptible to attack and degradation. High fever may also destroy fragile red blood cells, as will infections such as malaria.

A sub-type of haemolytic anaemia occurs when antibodies are produced which (erroneously) bind to red blood cells. This is therefore called autoimmune haemolytic anaemia. These autoantibodies will make the cells a target of the immune system and will lead to their elimination, often in the spleen. Indeed, a treatment for certain types of haemolytic anaemia includes splenectomy.

Red blood cells may be lost through an acute or chronic bleed. The former may include bleeding after surgery, heavy menstrual bleeding, or bleeding by a ruptured blood vessel that may leak into the intestines. If this process is occult, or prolonged, it may lead to a chronic state of blood loss. In these types of anaemia, there is nothing intrinsically wrong with the blood cells themselves.

The most common congenital haemoglobinopathies are sickle cell disease and thalassaemia, genetic conditions characterised by qualitative changes in the haemoglobin molecule that severely reduce its ability to transport oxygen. These cells also have a shorter lifespan than cells carrying normal haemoglobin, and both conditions are associated with a variety of clinical conditions such as jaundice and skin ulcers.

There are, of course, many more possible types of anaemia. The above, summarised in Table 2, simply lists major causes.

Table 2: A simple classification of anaemia

1. **Depressed red blood cell production from the bone marrow:**
   - Due to infiltrating cancer (e.g. leukaemia, or secondaries from other primary cancers elsewhere, such as the breast or prostate)
   - Due to total marrow shut-down (e.g. aplastic anaemia, or due to drugs, such as the chemotherapy used to treat cancer)
2. **Diet deficiency and organ disease**
   - Iron
   - Vitamin B_{12} and folate
   - Plasma proteins (for building essential carriage and storage molecules)
   - Liver and renal failure
3. **Loss of mature red blood cells**
   - Drugs causing haemolytic anaemia
   - Fevers, infections
   - Autoimmunity
   - Acute or chronic bleeding
4. **Haemoglobinopathy**
   - Sickle cell disease
   - Thalassaemia

A cautionary tale – 1

In the past there was great debate as to the definition of anaemia, such as the haemoglobin count being less than a pre-defined level of 80, 90, 100g/L or even (marginally) below the reference range. Consider this case report.

The case is a woman in her thirties with homozygous sickle cell disease. She was a fully trained pharmacist, had worked full-time, had one uneventful and successful pregnancy, and had never received a blood transfusion. When she was last seen at her local clinic in Jamaica, her haemoglobin was 39g/L. Was she anaemic?

In 1997 she emigrated to the USA, and two years later was seen routinely by her family doctor who found a haemoglobin result of 38 g/L. Again – was she anaemic? Her family doctor and colleagues apparently believed so, and she was transfused with six units of blood within 24 hours. This increased her haematocrit from 11% to 31%, but also increased her systolic and diastolic blood pressures by 30mmHg each. Nine hours after the last transfusion she reported a headache, subsequently developed cerebral haemorrhage, and later died.

I will not discuss this case further as, I believe, it is self-explanatory. However, the report concludes with '… the award of US$11.5 million recommended by the jury in this case could have been avoided'. Other comments on blood transfusion follow in Chapter 4.

Source: Serjeant, G. Blood transfusion in sickle cell disease: a cautionary tale. *Lancet* 2003, 361:1659–60.

Size matters!

The red cell index MCV can also be used to further classify anaemia. For example, in the anaemia that follows problems with vitamin B12, the red blood cells are larger than normal (e.g. greater than 98fL), and are said to be macrocytes. If the haemoglobin is low and the patient is symptomatic, they are therefore said to have macrocytic anaemia. Conversely, some haemoglobinopathies and iron-deficient states often lead to microcytic anaemia because the red blood cells are small (e.g. less than 80fL) and are called microcytes. Finally, a normocytic anaemia may be associated with a normal-sized red blood cell (a normocyte, between 80 and 98fL) but a lower overall haemoglobin level.

A prime reason for a normocytic anaemia will be the sudden loss of a large number of (healthy) red blood cells, perhaps through an accident, via a perforated duodenal ulcer, or bleeding gastrointestinal cancer. Here, there is nothing intrinsically wrong with the red cells themselves; the anaemia follows from another problem. Treatment therefore follows aetiology: more iron in the diet will not help an anaemia based on malabsorption, but intravenous iron may increase the haemoglobin level.

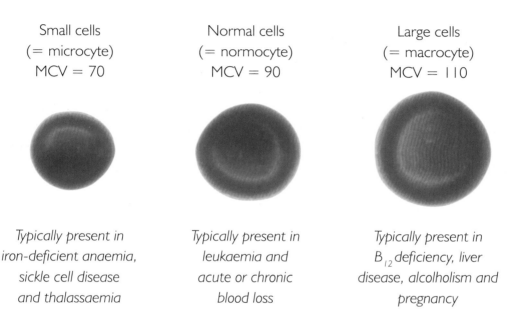

Small cells (= microcyte) MCV = 70	Normal cells (= normocyte) MCV = 90	Large cells (= macrocyte) MCV = 110
Typically present in iron-deficient anaemia, sickle cell disease and thalassaemia	*Typically present in leukaemia and acute or chronic blood loss*	*Typically present in B_{12} deficiency, liver disease, alcolholism and pregnancy*

Figure 2: Red cell size

This illustrates how the three red cell indices can vary. Taking the haemoglobin to be 130g/L and 4.5 x 10^{12}cells/mL in each of these cases with different MCVs, then the MCHC would be 412pg/L in the microcyte, 320pg/L in the normocyte and 262pg/L in the macrocyte. This may well be important in certain conditions.

Increased levels of red cell indices

Ideally, the healthy body tightly regulates the numbers and quality of the various aspects of the red blood cells. However, in rare instances, high levels are reported.

Polycythaemia is an excess overall red cell mass and is generally associated with a high haemoglobin, RBCC and haematocrit. This condition may arise from a rare kind of malignancy or over-activity of the bone marrow, and is more correctly called polycythaemia rubravera.

A second cause of increased red cell indices is because of the response of the bone marrow to reduced levels of oxygen, and is called erythrocytosis. This is understandable in those people living at a very high altitude (up mountains), where the air is very thin and of low oxygen content, but in the UK this cannot be the case.

The most common form of erythrocytosis is reactive to hypoxia, and (until recently) the dominant form of this was an unhealthy lifestyle with heavy smoking. A contributing factor is that tobacco smoke contains carbon monoxide, which binds irreversibly to haemoglobin and prevents it carrying oxygen, leading to poor oxygen-carrying capacity and thus a pseudo-anaemia. It is also possible that the low grade pulmonary damage caused by tobacco smoke causes poor oxygen movement across the alveoli. The bone marrow responds by producing high numbers of excess red blood cells in an attempt to improve (restore) oxygen-carrying capacity. Consequently, this places an extra strain on the heart and circulation. Fortunately, the reduction in the rate of smoking means that we are seeing less of this type of problem.

Possibly for the same reason (response to hypoxia), an increased red blood cell count can be seen in chronic anaemia such as thalassaemia, as the bone marrow attempts to improve the blood's ability to carry oxygen.

Recommended websites

www.hbregistry.org.uk/information/haemoglobinopathies.html

www.nhs.uk/conditions/Anaemia-iron-deficiency-/

www.pernicious-anaemia-society.org/

Summary of red blood cells

- Haemoglobin (Hb) is the key index used to investigate the major disease of red cells: anaemia.
- To aid precise diagnosis, the causes of the anaemia, and directions for treatment, RBCC, Hct and MCV are frequently referred to.
- Often less useful, but occasionally very enlightening, are MCH and MCHC.
- ESR and plasma viscosity are non-specific markers: an abnormal result could reflect a variety of different pathologies.
- The MCV tells us whether the anaemia is microcytic, normocytic or macrocytic, and so is likely to guide therapy.

Case study 1

A 20-year-old female and her family recently moved to this country from the Far East. Following a few weeks' acclimatisation and recovery from jet lag, it became clear to her family that she was consistently tired and lethargic (more so than her siblings) but had no symptoms of infection (e.g. a fever). Blood results were as follows.

	Result (unit)	Reference range
Haemoglobin	105g/L	118–148
RBCC	6.0 x 10^{12}/L	3.88–4.99
MCH	17.5pg	27.3–32.6
MCV	55fL	80–98
MCHC	318pg/L	316–349
Hct	0.33	0.36–0.44
ESR	9mm/hour	<10
Plasma viscosity	1.62mPa	1.5–1.72

Interpretation

The abnormal results are reduced haemoglobin, MCV, MCH and Hct, with a raised red cell count. The ESR and plasma viscosity are within the normal range but the ESR is close to abnormal. With a haemoglobin level below the bottom of the normal range of 118 for a young woman, and the symptoms, we would have little difficulty in describing her result as concerning, and would therefore probably label her as anaemic. Very heavy menstrual periods may possibly produce this picture, but as the red blood cells are not simply small (i.e. MCV <80), but are very small (<60), we have no hesitation in describing a microcytic anaemia, not an anaemia due to simple blood loss by itself. High numbers of red blood cells may well be a response to the oxygen-carrying problem.

The most common reasons for microcytic anaemia are iron deficiency, sickle cell disease and thalassaemia. Iron status can be easily tested for, and a test for sickle cell disease is also very simple to perform. However, both types of haemoglobinopathies are ultimately diagnosed by another test (chromatography, HPLC). Thus, with a normal iron profile and negative sickle test, thalassaemia would seem to be an appropriate diagnosis.

2

The white blood cell

Key words:

White blood cell count (WBCC)
The differential:
Neutrophils
Lymphocytes
Monocytes
Eosinophils
Basophils
Blasts/atypical cells

Key pathological expressions:

Leukocytosis and leukopenia
Leukaemia
Lymphoma and myeloma
Inflammation and immunity
Phagocytosis

An explanation of terms:

White blood cell count

White blood cells, or leukocytes, are collectively responsible for defending us from attack by micro-organisms such as viruses, bacteria and parasites, when raised levels of these cells can be expected. However, increased numbers may also be present in several conditions such as rheumatoid arthritis and cancer, and also after surgery and, as we shall see in detail, in leukaemia. Haematologists currently recognise five different types of white blood cells that can be found in the (normal) blood. The WBCC differential reports the numbers or proportions of these cells, which are neutrophils, lymphocytes, monocytes, eosinophils and basophils. There are also a few cells called blasts, or atypical cells.

The WBCC differential

This is the proportion of the different types of leukocytes. A typical report may be neutrophils 70%, lymphocytes 20%, monocytes 7%, eosinophils 2% and basophils <1% (see the reference range, page 142). However, in pathology, these proportions will be altered. The differential may also be reported as the absolute number of each type of cell. For example, if the WBCC is 7.5×10^9/L, then the number of lymphocytes will be 1.5×10^9/L if the differential, as above, is 20%. However, in a reaction to a virus, the lymphocyte count may rise four-fold, to, for example, 6×10^9/L. If all the other leukocytes remain the same, then total WBCC will have increased to 12×10^9/L, which is outside the normal range, and the proportion of lymphocytes will have increased to 50%, also above the reference range.

White blood cells

A blood film is made by smearing a drop of blood on a glass slide, and staining it with different dyes. Figure 3 shows an example of what you would see when viewing a blood film by light microscopy. The two larger bodies in the middle are white blood cells (characterised by a purple nucleus), surrounded by dozens of smaller red blood cells.

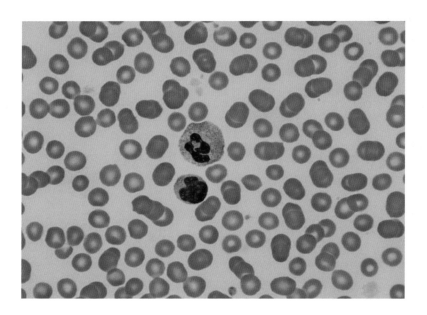

Figure 3: A blood film seen through a light microscope

Neutrophils (generally 40 to 75% of the WBCC)

These are the most common white cells, and are known as polymorphonuclear leukocytes (i.e. many different [irregular] shapes, usually three to five), granulocytes (i.e. with granules in the cytoplasm), or simply as polymorphs. The upper cell in Figure 3 is a neutrophil. However, basophils and eosinophils also have an irregular nucleus and have granules, so others may consider these cells also to be polymorphs and granulocytes.

Lymphocytes (20 to 45% of the WBCC)

The second most common group of white cells, lymphocytes differ principally from neutrophils in the structure of their nucleus, which is round and regular (in contrast to the neutrophil's numerous irregular shapes). Lymphocytes are also normally smaller than neutrophils, and don't have granules. The lower cell in Figure 3 is a lymphocyte.

Monocytes (2 to 10% of the WBCC)

These cells often resemble lymphocytes, as they also have a round, regular nucleus. However, the nucleus of most monocytes does not take up as much of the cell (maybe up to 80%,) whereas the lymphocyte nucleus frequently occupies over 95% of the cell. Monocytes are also larger than lymphocytes. It is often suggested that many monocytes are only temporarily in the blood, on their way to the tissues where they reside.

Eosinophils (1 to 6% of the WBCC)

These cells are so-called because they readily absorb reddish eosin dye, due to the chemical make-up of their granules. The nucleus is of composed of just two parts, linked together by a small thread.

Basophils (less than 1% of the WBCC)

The least frequent of the normal leukocytes, basophils contain numerous granules that take up different dyes, and so appear as black or dark blue. They resemble eosinophils in size and nuclear shape, but are not red.

Blasts/atypical cells (less than 1% of the WBCC)

There will generally be great agreement amongst haematologists about definitions of the five major sub-types of white blood cells. However, occasionally the odd cell appears in the blood that defies this simple classification. Such cells, often with unusual characteristics, may be described as blasts or atypical cells.

In certain clear disease, as will be outlined below, increased numbers of blasts carry pathological implications, some of which are profound. For example, in several types of acute leukaemia, the abnormal cells have such a strange morphology that they are described as blasts, and can be of the lymphoid or neutrophil family.

What are white cells for?

As previously indicated, white cells are responsible for defending us from attack by micro-organisms, and they are also involved in repair and reconstruction following tissue damage. The main function of **neutrophils** is to defend us from pathogenic micro-organisms (bacteria and viruses), and they do this by ingesting them, a process known as **phagocytosis**. Indeed, neutrophils may also be known as phagocytes. Consequently, high numbers of neutrophils are often associated with bacterial infections, but may also be found in autoimmune diseases. This is because in autoimmune disease, such as arthritis, the immune and inflammatory systems foolishly decide to attack the body's own tissues (such as the skin and joints) instead of bacteria. Autoimmunity is explained in Chapter 5. Increased white cell levels in the absence of an infection, such as after surgery or severe exercise, may be explained as part of the body's normal response to physical stress, the so-called 'acute phase response'. Such raised levels can be expected to fall back to normal as the cause of the stress subsides.

Whilst many **lymphocytes** are present in the blood, they are mainly present in lymph nodes, the bone marrow, the liver and the spleen. These organs are collectively called 'lymphoid tissue'. Mildly increased numbers of lymphocytes in the blood may be expected in conditions that also cause a raised neutrophil count. However, the highest levels often encountered in health are found during attack against viral infections, such as glandular fever, which is also known as infectious mononucleosis. In such cases, these 'activated' lymphocytes may be larger than usual, and sufficiently larger for them to be described as blasts. However, some viruses actually kill lymphocytes, in which case the number in the blood will fall – HIV being such a virus.

Monocytes also defend us from infection by the phagocytosis of bacteria, fungi and other pathogens, but this also occurs in tissues such as the skin, liver and lung, where they are described as macrophages. In addition, monocytes co-operate with lymphocytes in making antibodies, and increased numbers of monocytes can be present in chronic bacterial and protozoal infections, and in malignancy.

The last two types of normal cells are present at low levels. **Eosinophils** defend us against infection by large parasites, and are also active in allergy, hay fever, asthma and skin diseases. High numbers of **basophils** are rare but may be present in acute hypersensitivity and atopic reactions, and in some leukaemias.

Inflammation and immunity

Thus neutrophils, lymphocytes and monocytes defend us from microbial pathogens. This type of defence can be viewed as having two parts: inflammatory and immunity:

- An inflammatory response often sees a large number of neutrophils being rapidly mobilised to attack a localised bacterial infection, although such a local response may escape into the blood and lead to septicaemia. Unfortunately, these neutrophils can be a little too 'enthusiastic' and local tissues may be damaged or destroyed in addition to the pathogens.
- There are two major types of lymphocytes: B lymphocytes make immunoglobulins (antibodies, which are proteins designed to recognise, attack, and help destroy invading pathogens), whilst T lymphocytes co-operate in antibody production and also attack cells that are infected with viruses such as influenza, measles and the viruses that cause hepatitis. These responses may take several days to reach peak efficiency.

Although they are two different processes, inflammatory and immune responses often co-operate. A good example of this is the symbiosis between the two most common types of white blood cells. Lymphocytes may make antibodies to bacteria and fungi such as yeast, which are then more palatable to the phagocytic neutrophils and monocytes, thus aiding removal of these pathogens. For a full and comprehensive defence against micro-organisms, both inflammatory and immunological mechanisms are therefore required. Infections occur when either, or both, of these processes become impaired.

Antibodies are not always good, as they can take part in autoimmune diseases such as rheumatoid arthritis and thyroiditis, and often frustrate our wish to give or receive a blood transfusion (Chapter 4).

Not enough cells: leukopenia

This state is often described when the white cell count falls to less than, for example, 3.7×10^9/L. However, we need to bear in mind that the definition of the reference range may well include some individuals with leukopenia who are entirely healthy. Nevertheless, persistently low levels are very rare in the absence of a clear explanation. Many people of African descent have low white cell numbers: This can be entirely normal.

In clinical practice, virtually all cases of leukopenia are associated with the use of certain cytotoxic drugs such as the ones used in the treatment of solid cancers, leukaemia, and to aid the success of a transplant. These drugs, many of which are effectively sophisticated poison, can cause the destruction of different types of white blood cells. However, low numbers of neutrophils (i.e. neutropenia) can also be associated with supposedly benign drugs such as anti-inflammatory medication. In such cases, the cause is therefore reasonably apparent. It follows that prophylactic antibiotic therapy is often needed in such patients. Other drugs can cause the selective loss of lymphocytes (i.e. lymphopenia), and these individuals may then be at risk of viral infections.

As discussed earlier, low levels of white blood cells are also to be found in aplastic anaemia (a condition where the entire bone marrow shuts down), and so a low WBCC is also associated with anaemia and low numbers of platelets.

High numbers of cells: leukocytosis

As previously mentioned, high levels of neutrophils and lymphocytes can be found as normal responses to infections and after surgery. The reason for the former is obvious, but the latter is an example of an acute phase response – the body believes it has been attacked, and therefore mobilises white blood cells in case it needs to defend itself from a bacterial infection.

Pathological states also associated with leukocytosis include inflammatory and autoimmune diseases such as rheumatoid arthritis and systemic lupus erythematosus. However, the highest and most serious cases of leukocytosis occur in leukaemia.

Leukaemia

The high white cell count in leukaemia is not due to an abnormal or persistent response to infections, but to changes in the ways in which white blood cells develop in the bone marrow. Essentially, the leukaemic cells stop their development at a certain crucial but early stage, and enter the blood not only in an immature state, but also in increased numbers. If this process develops slowly, perhaps over years, then it is said to be chronic, with survival measurable in years. These leukaemic cells are often of a more mature phenotype.

Conversely, if the increase in the white cell count is rapid, maybe over a few weeks, then the leukaemia is said to be acute. Acute leukaemias, frequently characterised by enormous numbers of immature cells (also called blasts), are also often much more aggressive than the chronic counterpart, where the increases are more modest, and survival (unless treated appropriately) can be as short as months.

If the major cell in the leukaemia is of the neutrophil lineage, the leukaemia is described as myeloid. When the predominant cell is a lymphocyte, then lymphocytic leukaemia is present. However, if the leukaemia is dominated by blast cells, then it may be described as lymphoblastic. Thus, for the most common leukaemias, we have a combination of these in abbreviations:

- AML = acute myeloid leukaemia
- CML = chronic myeloid leukaemia
- ALL = acute lymphoblastic leukaemia
- CLL = chronic lymphocytic leukaemia

Monocytic leukaemias are rare, whilst eosinophil and basophil leukaemias are very rare indeed. Myeloid and lymphocytic leukaemias therefore provide by far the most work of this kind for the haematologist.

Because the leukaemia arises in the bone marrow, and is characterised by large numbers of these abnormal cells, the production of other cells within this tissue is also influenced. Thus anaemia and low levels of platelets (thrombocytopenia) are invariably a consequence of leukaemia, as the tumour grows and squeezes out other normal tissues. In advanced disease, the leukaemia may escape from the bone marrow and will often invade lymphoid tissues of the lymph nodes, liver and spleen, making them swollen. These conditions are called lymphadenopathy, hepatomegaly and splenomegaly respectively.

Treatments are aimed at reducing the tumour burden, and generally involve regimes of cytotoxic drugs. More severe leukaemias demand transplantation of fresh, 'clean' bone marrow stem cells that can be obtained from a donor (i.e. allogeneic, best from an HLA-matched donor) or from the patient themselves (i.e. an autologous transplant).

The natural history of leukaemia

We all experience minor fluctuations in blood results from day to day and week to week – hence the slight variation in the white cell line. Indeed, levels can rise with 'normal' responses to infection, up to levels in the 'teens, say 14 or 15. However, as the white cell count continues to rise to about 20 or 25 without an obvious infection (with symptoms of fevers and sweating), then a malignancy becomes likely.

An increased white cell count is present in almost all cases of leukaemia, but may also be due to an infection. Figure 4 illustrates these points – the vertical axis is the cell count and the horizontal axis, time. The solid grey lines are the upper limit of normal (ULN) and lower limit of normal (LLN).

The white cell count is generally very stable over time but will rise markedly and rapidly in an acute infection (point A), often going above the top of the reference range, but will return to normal once the infection has passed. The red cell count (dashed line) and platelet count (dotted line) are not changed by this infection.

By far the most common cause of leukaemia is radiation causing a mutation in the DNA of a stem cell in the bone marrow (point B). This is followed by steady rise in the white cell count as leukaemic white cells leave the bone marrow for the blood. These cells are immature, and provide reduced defence against micro-organisms, leading to infections, such as at time point C. A full blood count taken at this point will find a raised white cell count, but red cell and platelet counts are still within the reference range.

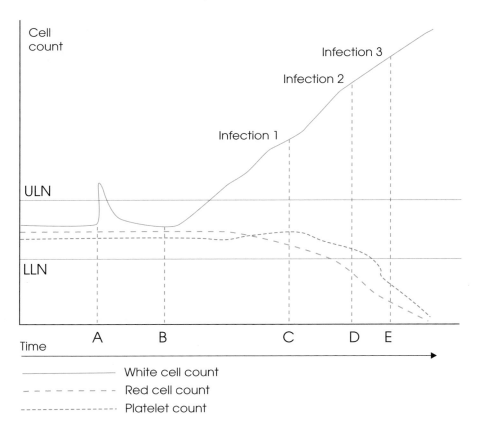

Figure 4: How blood cell levels change as leukaemia progresses

As the leukaemic tumour within the bone marrow grows, the white cell count continues to rise and more infections follow. At the second, point D, the red cell count is below the bottom of the reference range, but the platelet count is still in range. As the disease progresses, these other cell counts inevitably fall below the bottom of their reference ranges (point E) and the patient is likely to experience symptoms of anaemia and thrombocytopenia, such as tiredness and lethargy, and bruising and bleeding respectively.

This brings us to Table 3, which summarises the key points of leukaemia, from both the patient's perspective and that of the laboratory. It is not necessary to see all six conditions fulfilled, but if they are, the diagnosis is unquestionable.

Table 3: Diagnosis of leukaemia

	Patient factor	Laboratory factor
Red cells	Tiredness, lethargy, etc (i.e. the symptoms of anaemia)	Low haemoglobin, low red cell count
White cells	Infections	High white cell count
Platelets	Bruising, bleeding	Low platelet count (thrombocytopenia)

Differential diagnoses of leukaemia

The single most defining characteristic of leukaemia is a raised white cell count, but this may also be present in severe infections. The most dangerous and life-threatening type of infection is septicaemia (blood poisoning), where the blood itself is infected with bacteria, which will be confirmed by blood culture. A patient with septicaemia is likely to be in an intensive care unit, with a high temperature and tachycardia, and will probably be on industrial doses of intravenous antibiotics.

The white cell count of such a patient is likely to be in the region of 20, perhaps 25×10^9 cells/mL, and over 90% of these are likely to be neutrophils. It follows that a patient, maybe feeling poorly and with a persistent cough and a white cell count greater than 25×10^9 cells/mL, is most unlikely to have septicaemia (especially if most of the white cells are lymphocytes). Instead, they are likely to be in the early stages of leukaemia. However, this rule is far from perfect, and the occasional patient presents with a very high white cell count in the absence of either septicaemia or leukaemia.

Other lymphoid neoplasia

Whilst leukaemia arises in the bone marrow, other types of lymphoid malignancy can be present in other lymphoid tissues around the body, such as the liver, spleen and lymph nodes.

Lymphoma

This disease is a cancer of mostly B lymphocytes or, rarely, T lymphocytes. Essentially, malignant but inactive lymphocytes take over the normal structure and function of the lymph node. As these small organs are often the sites of antibody production, they are no longer able to help fight infection. The principal example of this type of cancer is a Hodgkin or non-Hodgkin lymphoma; another is a Burkitt's lymphoma, though the latter can also be caused by a virus.

Lymphomas are often progressive: more and more lymph nodes, often in a chain, become affected, and eventually the spleen, liver and bone marrow (thereby possibly leading to anaemia) can become involved. Lymphoma cells are not usually seen in the blood, so a leukocytosis is infrequent. However, a lymphoma may well deteriorate in its later stages into a disease with a leukaemic picture in the blood.

Important differential diagnoses of lymphoma are self-limiting cases of lymphadenopathy as may occur in tonsillitis, downstream of an infected wound, and in a clear viral infection such as mumps.

Myeloma

This is a tumour of the B lymphocyte that is (normally) making good antibodies to attack bacteria and viruses. However, unlike a lymphoma, this tumour is found within the bone marrow. The disease, accounting for maybe 10% of all haematological malignancies, and with a median survival of four years, can cause bone pain, and often so much bone is mobilised that serum calcium can rise. As the myeloma cells are making large amounts of an incorrect type of antibody, the viscosity of the blood rises. A further consequence of this is a very high erythrocyte sedimentation rate (ESR).

Although centred on the bone marrow, the actual tumour cells of the myeloma (plasma cells) can be found in the blood, especially in advanced disease. A myeloma may therefore start out (and possibly remain) centred on the bone marrow, but these myeloma cells may 'escape' (or be pushed out) into the blood and/or lymph nodes. However, numbers hardly ever rise to those of a 'typical' leukaemia.

Myeloma is ultimately diagnosed by very high levels of serum immunoglobulins (antibodies), using a test called protein electrophoresis, often performed in the Biochemistry Laboratory. In some cases, only a small part of the quite large antibody molecule is produced in excess amounts, and this can be detected in the blood or in the urine. This fraction of an entire antibody molecule is called 'Bence Jones Protein' after Henry Bence Jones, the physician who discovered it.

Recommended websites

www.cancerresearchuk.org/leukaemia

www.lymphoma.org.uk

www.myeloma.org.uk

Summary of white blood cells

- White blood cells defend us from infections, when raised levels of these cells can be found in the blood.
- Increased numbers of neutrophils are found in bacterial infection.
- Viral infections are characterised by high numbers of lymphocytes.
- The most serious disease associated with inappropriately high WBC levels is leukaemia, a condition where anaemia and low platelets are also often present.
- Other cancers of white blood cells are lymphoma and myeloma.

Case study 2

A 20-year-old student presented a week after the onset of influenza-like symptoms, with general malaise, sweating, pyrexia, an intermittent skin rash and a sore throat. As the symptoms seemed to be more severe and persistent than would be consistent with general flu, a blood test was performed:

	Result (unit)	Reference range
WCC	12.1×10^9/L	3.7–9.5
Neutrophils	4.4×10^9/L	1.7–6.1
Lymphocytes	6.6×10^9/L	1.0–3.2
Monocytes	0.35×10^9/L	0.2–0.6
Eosinophils	0.25×10^9/L	0.03–0.46
Basophils	0.05×10^9/L	0.02–0.09
Blasts	0.45×10^9/L	<0.01

Interpretation

The initial abnormality is a raised white cell count. This justifies the differential, which reports a lymphocytosis but also increased blasts. The primary cause of a lymphocytosis is a viral infection.

Notably, the number of blasts exceeds that of the monocytes, which cannot be physiological. However, these are not true malignant blasts, but are simply atypical lymphocytes, perhaps activated by the acute phase response and so seeking other cells that are infected with viruses. A likely primary diagnosis is infectious mononucleosis, which can be confirmed by the Paul Bunnell/Monospot test. Treatment is symptomatic – that is, bed rest, fluids and analgesia.

3

Coagulation

Key words:

Platelets
Fibrinogen
Prothrombin time (PT)
Partial thromboplastin time (PTT)
International normalised ratio (INR)

Key pathological expressions:

Thrombocytopenia
Thrombocytosis
Haemorrhage
Thrombosis
Antithrombotic drugs
Anticoagulant drugs

An explanation of terms:

Platelets

These tiny bodies are fragments of a much larger cell found only in the bone marrow (the megakaryocyte), and form a clot, or thrombus, when aggregated together with the help of the blood protein fibrin. A low platelet count (possibly caused by drugs such as quinine, sulphonamides and other antibiotics, or poor production, or excessive consumption) is thrombocytopenia. A raised count is thrombocytosis, and this is often present in infections and some autoimmune diseases.

Fibrinogen

This is one of the more important blood proteins involved in clotting and is made in the liver.

It is converted into fibrin by an enzyme, thrombin (which is itself derived from prothrombin), and is crucial in clot formation. Increased levels of fibrin are found in inflammation and in smokers, and decreased levels due to consumption when forming a clot.

Prothrombin time (PT) and partial thromboplastin time (PTT)

The PT and PTT are laboratory measures of the plasma's ability to form a clot, and they can be used to investigate bleeding disorders. The result provided is the time taken (in the laboratory, not in the body) for the clot to form. The difference between PT and PTT is that they measure different parts of the clotting pathway. They can also be used to monitor the effects of different drugs that interfere with different parts of the coagulation system. PT is used to measure the anticoagulant warfarin; and PTT is used to measure heparin. Some labs place an 'A' for 'activated' in front of the PTT, thus APTT.

International normalised ratio (INR)

The most widely used anticoagulant that can be given by mouth is warfarin. It works by interfering with the liver's ability to synthesise proteins involved in clotting, so that clotting takes longer to happen in the laboratory. The INR is simply the ratio between the time blood takes to clot normally, compared to the (supposedly increased) time it takes to clot due to warfarin. For example, if a normal clotting time (PT) is 12 seconds, and on warfarin the time is 24 seconds, then the INR is 2.0. We use the INR to strike a balance between slowing down the clot-forming process, and the use of too much warfarin, which will interfere with clotting so much that a clot may never form (a dangerous situation to be in!).

Someone at a relatively low risk of thrombosis (for example, with atrial fibrillation), or with a current deep vein thrombosis (DVT) should have an INR between 2 and 3. However, those at high risk of thrombosis (for example, with a mechanical heart valve), or someone who seems to be predisposed to clots, would generally be expected to take enough warfarin to maintain an INR between 3 and 4.

What is coagulation for?

The coagulation system exists to prevent excessive blood loss. A clot is composed of two elements: platelets and fibrin. Imagine a small river or stream that you need to dam. One approach would be to throw a tennis net over the steam, and then float down footballs, tennis balls, basketballs, etc. Eventually, the flow of water would be impeded. In this simple metaphor, the tennis net is the fibrin, and the various balls are platelets, red blood cells and white blood cells. Clearly, the tennis net by itself would not stop much water flow, and footballs by themselves would simply be washed away. They have to work together to stop water flow, just as platelets and fibrin work together to form a clot. The tennis balls and footballs metaphor is far from perfect (in real life, the balls would not take an active part in stopping water flow). But platelets are in fact very active cells, and they do take a direct part in supporting the fibrin net and making the clot more stable.

The key to understanding thrombosis and haemostasis is the coagulation cascade. This is like a waterfall, in which a host of different coagulation molecules come together, to activate each other, and form thrombin. This converts fibrinogen to fibrin, which forms a clot with platelets (see Figure 5). This pathway is important because it shows us how to inhibit the process of thrombus formation using anticoagulants.

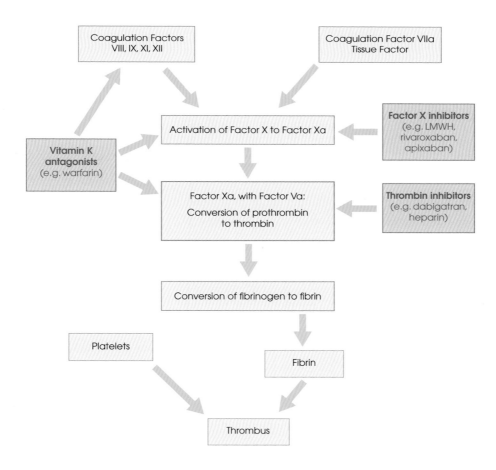

Figure 5: The coagulation cascade

The causes, consequences and treatments of increased tendency to form a clot

As the proper word for a clot is a thrombus, the process that concludes with the formation of a clot is known as thrombosis. This can occur in the arteries or in the veins.

Clots in arteries

The consequence of an arterial thrombosis that totally blocks the artery is an infarction. In this case, the tissues downstream of the clot die because they are deprived of oxygen and glucose. If the clot lies in an artery within the heart, a (possibly fatal) myocardial infarction (heart attack) therefore follows. Similarly, a clot in an artery in the brain will cause a stroke. Clots in the legs will cause critical limb ischaemia, as well as considerable pain and, possibly, the development of gangrene. These thromboses are the mainstay of atherothrombotic disease, which seems to affect the majority of people in the Western world as they get older. Most people are aware of the importance of the risk factors for atherosclerosis (diabetes, smoking, hypertension and hypercholesterolaemia), which all promote clot formation.

Clots in veins

When a clot forms in a vein, it is termed a venous thromboembolism (VTE). The principal vessels burdened are in the legs (where a deep vein thrombosis [DVT] can develop) and in the lungs (where a pulmonary embolus [PE] may arise). Other veins, such as those in the arm and shoulder, are rarely burdened. A DVT leads to a painful, red and inflamed leg, which means that walking can be difficult, if not impossible. Blood flow is impeded, and the leg can become swollen by tissue fluid. DVT is not directly life-threatening in itself, but if the clot breaks up, particles (emboli) can pass into the circulation and cause problems elsewhere. This can lead to the blockage of a crucial lung vessel (PE), which will lead to breathlessness and chest pain, and can be fatal. The major risk factors for VTE include surgery (especially orthopaedic), cancer and obesity.

There are several major drugs that are useful for those at risk of, and needing treatment for, thrombosis.

Aspirin

This is certainly the most commonly used drug for the treatment and prevention of arterial thrombosis. It is effective and cheap, does not require refrigeration, and one dose (75mg daily) for all can be given orally. It is now a standard treatment for anyone who has already had a critical cardiovascular event. It works by reducing platelet activity, so these cells don't get as enthusiastic about forming a clot.

Clopidogrel

Despite its success, some people are intolerant of, or resistant to, aspirin. These individuals therefore need other drugs, such as clopidogrel, to suppress their platelets. The standard dose is again 75mg daily. This drug works in a different way to aspirin, and the two are often used together after a stroke, heart attack or the placement of an intra-cardiac stent.

Warfarin

Vitamin K, normally obtained in our diet, is an essential requirement for our ability to synthesise key molecules involved in coagulation. If our diet is deficient in this vitamin, we can't make the coagulation factors as efficiently and so we don't form clots that well. Warfarin works by inhibiting this synthesis activity, resulting in low levels of clotting proteins and a correspondingly long time to form a clot. This gives some protection from thrombosis.

As we have seen, the INR is a simple number that compares the time taken for the blood to clot whilst an individual is on warfarin, compared with the time when they are not on the drug. Despite its excellent efficacy, warfarin's use is plagued by the risk of bleeding and by the variability of the dose required by different people. Some may only need 1mg a day, whilst others have to take 15mg daily to make their blood equally anticoagulated. Consequently, most patients need to attend a monthly outpatient clinic to check that they are taking the right amount of warfarin for their particular INR. One serious but rare side effect of warfarin is skin necrosis, which often demands surgery.

Heparin

Heparin is a natural anticoagulant – we all have it in our blood. However, giving extra heparin will help those at risk of thrombosis – for instance, immediately after orthopaedic surgery. A disadvantage with this agent is that it can't be taken by mouth, so must be given by subcutaneous injection, or intravenously. A further problem is that it can cause dangerously low levels of platelets, leading to excessive bleeding, a condition called heparin-induced thrombocytopenia. If this happens, heparin is withdrawn and another anticoagulant, such as hirudin (derived from the leech), can be used instead. Like warfarin, the efficacy of heparin can vary from person to person, so it must be monitored in the laboratory using the PTT test.

Low molecular weight heparin (LMWH)

This is a safer form of old-style unfractionated heparin. Although it cannot be taken orally, LMWH is safe enough to be given by subcutaneous injection, even in outpatient clinics and (for the appropriately trained patient) at home, and does not need to be monitored by the PTT test. There is also a reduced incidence of heparin-induced thrombocytopenia. There is now a form of LMWH that needs to be given only once a week.

New oral anticoagulants (NOACs)

This group consists of two types of drug: one type that directly inhibits thrombin (dabigatran), and another type that inhibits Factor Xa (rivaroxaban and apixaban). These drugs are at least as effective and have better safety profiles (some more so) than warfarin for the prevention of stroke in atrial fibrillation. They are also preferable to LMWH for the prevention of DVT and PE after orthopaedic surgery. Some have, or are likely to have, licences for the prevention and treatment of DVT and PE in a medical setting.

As they do not require monitoring with a blood test, these agents are set to replace warfarin and LMWH in many conditions. Indeed, several are licensed for use in the prevention of stroke in atrial fibrillation, and the prevention of venous thrombosis after orthopaedic surgery. Other indications are likely to follow.

Anticoagulation management

As healthcare professionals, we focus on prevention and treatment. All patients coming into hospital must have their risk of VTE assessed, and if it is high enough, prophylactic treatment should be given. This is likely to be a LMWH, as it is easy to handle, but in the future one of the NOACs may be used. The practitioner is strongly advised to refer to NICE guidelines.

From a practical point of view, patients coming out of surgery (and therefore at risk of thrombosis) need to be anticoagulated immediately. Historically, this has been done using a double approach of warfarin and a LMWH. This is necessary because LMWH acts almost immediately, whereas warfarin takes several days to become effective and thus protect against a clot. Once the INR has reached its target (generally 2–3), heparin may be withdrawn. However, this approach is rapidly falling out of favour, and many practitioners are now giving their patients one of the NOACs instead of this combination of LMWH and warfarin.

Alternatively, other patients may be protected by LMWH alone whilst in hospital and then be discharged with their own supply so they can dose themselves at home. Self-dosing is becoming attractive, as there is a long history of people with diabetes confidently and safely dosing themselves with insulin. However, this approach is also being superseded by the use of NOACs.

Atrial fibrillation (AF) is a major cause of stroke, and in such cases prophylaxis must be given. In the past, this has been warfarin to target INR 2–3. However, this is one area where NOACs may now be used with confidence.

All these antithrombotic and anticoagulant drugs have side effects (principally haemorrhage) when used in excess or in other situations. As mentioned earlier, unfractionated heparin can cause a thrombocytopenia and warfarin a skin necrosis.

The causes, consequences and treatments of reduced ability to form a clot

Haemorrhage is the medical term for bleeding, and we have noted that excessive anticoagulation with heparin, aspirin and warfarin can cause minor bleeding (e.g. bruising or nosebleeds) or more serious bleeding (with blood loss so severe that it may demand a blood transfusion). Fortunately, bleeding due to aspirin and heparin can often be managed by withdrawing the drug. However, as the effects of warfarin are long lasting, the antidote is to give vitamin K orally or by injection.

The best-known coagulation gene defect is haemophilia. This is caused by lack of a certain crucial component of the coagulation system, Factor VIII. Without this factor, bleeding is frequent. Fortunately, the disease is rare and, although always serious, is becoming easier to treat by giving replacements of Factor VIII that are made using genetic engineering. This revolutionary technology can also provide other clotting factors, such as recombinant Factor VII, which can be used to treat a variety of bleeding disorders.

The most common inherited bleeding disorder is von Willebrand's disease, which is caused by lack of von Willebrand factor. Unlike haemophilia, this condition is very variable, ranging from virtually asymptomatic to life threatening. If recombinant clotting factors are unavailable, excessive bleeding and haemorrhage can be treated with fresh frozen plasma or cryoglobulins, which are purified and prepared from blood transfusion donations. Transfusion of purified platelets is also possible, and these are generally taken from a blood bank. This is reviewed in Chapter 4, which discusses blood transfusion.

Fibrinolysis and D-dimers

Although these notes are designed to answer questions about the 'routine' full blood count, it is foolish to ignore other closely related and important topics merely because they do not yet appear on routine report forms.

Once a clot has formed, and has done its job in stemming blood loss, it must be removed by a process called fibrinolysis. The enzyme plasmin degrades the clot into small pieces so that blood flow can be restored. Plasmin derives from an inactive precursor, plasminogen, by the activity of tissue plasminogen activator (tPA). The current treatment of a heart attack, which is presumed to follow from a clot in one of the arteries of the heart, is to give tPa (or a closely related product such as streptokinase or alteplase) to help get rid of the clot that is causing the obstruction and associated symptoms.

D-dimers and VTE

A consequence of fibrinolysis is the appearance of bits of chopped-up clots in the plasma. These can be detected in the laboratory, and, of these fragments, D-dimers are the most useful. Thus, increased D-dimers are evidence of fibrinolysis, and so of the presence of a clot being resolved. DVT is caused by a clot in one of the veins in the leg. Resolution of the DVT by the body's own repair mechanisms should therefore be accompanied by raised levels of D-dimers. The trouble is that many conditions (including cancer, diabetes, smoking and atherosclerosis) are also accompanied by raised D-dimers, so the test is not specific for a DVT. Conversely, this test can also be used to exclude a DVT, as it is just about impossible to have normal D-dimers levels and a DVT.

Recommended websites

www.nice.org.uk/guidance

www.rcn.org.uk › ... › Nursing practice issues › CPD online learning

www.haemophilia.org.uk/

Summary

- The coagulation system exists to minimise blood loss by creating a clot (thrombus) to plug the hole.
- The clot is composed of platelets in a mesh of fibrin, which may also include red blood cells.
- Excessive and inappropriate clotting can lead to possibly fatal disease, and can be retarded by drugs such as aspirin, warfarin and heparin. The latter two are being superseded by the new oral anticoagulants (NOACs).
- Fibrinolysis is the dissolution of the clot, and leads to raised D-dimers (molecules that can be used to exclude a DVT).

Case study 3

The wife of a 65-year-old man who has recently returned home after a hip replacement calls the GP's surgery to say he has been having a lot of nose bleeds. You advise him to come in for a full blood count and coagulation screen. He does so, and the blood goes off to the Pathology Lab, who call you back to say that the results are normal, except for a platelet count of 75 x 10^9/L (reference range 150–400 x 10^9/L).

The patient has thrombocytopenia (low platelets). This is probably due to the use of a LMWH to reduce the risk of a VTE after orthopaedic surgery (hence heparin-induced thrombocytopenia). There are specialist tests to confirm this, but for the time being he needs to stop the LMWH, and be given either a direct thrombin inhibitor (such as argatroban) or one of the NOACs.

4

Blood transfusion

Key words:

ABO blood groups
Rh blood groups
Blood components
Antibodies
Antigens
Cross-match
Group and Save

Key pathological expressions:

Anaemia
Transfusion reaction

Introduction

A blood transfusion is clearly not a blood test. However, it is included in this book because it is an important therapy that practitioners need to be aware of, and may even consider in the management of their patients. This is not merely because the objective of blood transfusion has changed markedly over the years, from being a crude instrument to maintain the haemoglobin level, to a therapy to save lives. Another big change has been the realisation that this is far from a simple and trouble-free treatment. It is in fact a treatment that can damage, possibly permanently, the health of the recipient.

A further development has been the move from transfusing 'whole' blood, which therefore included plasma (with all its proteins and antibodies), white blood cells and platelets, to transfusing only specific components, usually just the red blood cells. The latter, called 'packed cells', is not only more efficient, but also, without the white blood cells and (possibly damaging) plasma antibodies, produces fewer adverse reactions. Furthermore, the 'leftover' plasma for a blood donation can provide other useful blood components (such as clotting proteins) although these can also be produced by genetic engineering.

Each blood group system (of which there are several) consists of two parts:

- Firstly, there are molecules that are present at the surface of the cells. These define blood groups, and are known as antigens.
- The second aspect is a series of antibodies that recognise the antigen molecules.

The interaction between these two aspects frustrates the lab scientists who try to match the antigens and antibodies of the patient with those of the blood provided by the donor.

An explanation of terms:

The ABO system

Antigens A and B are found on the surface of red blood cells. If you have only the blood group A structure on your red blood cells, you are blood group A. Similarly, if you have only group B molecules on your red cells then you are group B. People with both A and B molecules on their red blood cells are group AB, and if you have neither of these structures on your red cells, you are group O.

We also have antibodies in our plasma that recognise blood group structures A and B. But in the healthy individual, these are the reverse of your blood group. If you are group A, you will therefore have antibodies that will recognise group B (i.e. Anti-B). Likewise, group B people have antibodies that recognise group A (i.e. Anti-A). Group AB people have no antibodies, but group O people have both anti-A and anti-B antibodies. This is summarised in Table 4.

Table 4: Determinants of ABO blood group

Blood group frequency (%)	Antigen structures on the red cell surface	Antibodies in the plasma
40	A	Anti-B
8	B	Anti-B
3	AB	None
45	None, hence Group O	Anti-A and anti-B

The Rhesus system

The Rhesus (Rh) system is much more complicated, being composed of dozens of different antigens (although on a day-to-day basis, only five different structures on the surface of the red cell are commonly dealt with in the blood bank). A full explanation of this is beyond the scope of this book, but in practice we tend to focus on the molecule known as D (i.e. Rh D), as it is this structure and the antibodies it can generate that can give rise to haemolytic disease of the newborn (HDN) if not correctly treated. About 85% of white Europeans are Rh D+ve. Other members of the Rh family of antigens are C, c, E and e.

The main distinction between the ABO and Rh systems is that, in the normal person, there are *always* A and B antibodies to absent antigens. This makes ABO incompatibility potentially fatal.

Group and Save

The practitioner requests the laboratory to 'Group and Save' the patient's blood. The laboratory scientists determine the patient's ABO and Rh blood group (Group), but then keep the blood handy (Save, generally in a refrigerator), as it is likely to be needed in a Cross-match in the near future. The same blood is also screened for potential antibodies in the patient's blood that may cause problems later on. A Group and Save is often requested for patients who will be undergoing surgery in the next few days or weeks, so that the laboratory has a head start in trying to match some stored blood for them.

Cross-match

This is the second step, and is requested when the practitioner is absolutely convinced that the patient must be transfused, and a second blood sample will need to be taken. In an emergency (such as a massive haemorrhage after a road traffic accident), the 'Group and Save' and the 'Cross-match' may happen at the same time.

In practice, the blood bank staff oversee the mixing of blood from the patient (recipient) with a series of stored bloods (up to five or six) from different donors, to see if there are any matches. This is often done in an analyser. In a good match, the red blood cells are unaltered by this mixing, and therefore should not react when in the patient. However, blood that does not match will aggregate, forming small clots, indicating an incompatibility. This is inevitably because the antigens on the red blood cells and the antibodies in the serum recognise each other, and react together, causing blood to clump. It is presumed that the same reaction may happen in the blood vessels: the mixture is incompatible, and the donor pack cannot be given to the patient.

An example of this would be mixing blood from a group A individual with that of someone from blood group B. The group A person has group A molecules on their red cells but also antibodies against B in the plasma (i.e. Anti-B). The group B person has the reverse – group B molecules on their red cells and anti-A antibodies in their plasma. When mixed, the group A red cells will therefore be recognised by the anti-A antibodies, and so will react together. Similarly, the group B red blood cells will be recognised by the anti-B, and will also react. As we saw in Chapter 2 (page 23), the purpose of antibodies is often to attack and destroy anything they react with – hence the danger.

The same principle of incompatibility occurs in other systems, such as antibodies to an Rh antigen or to a Kell antigen being reactive with specific anti-Rh or anti-Kell antibodies.

Blood components

The blood pack itself is only red cells (hence 'packed cells'). The donor's plasma has been taken off, and components are prepared from its blood. Most of these components are used to help with haemorrhage (being rich in coagulation factors, such as prothrombin complex concentrate, and cryoglobulin), but there are also packs of albumin and platelets.

Why order a blood transfusion?

Firstly, the practitioner will ask: does the patient *really* need it? Are there any alternatives? For example, will erythropoietin do the trick? Is autologous transfusion possible? One textbook suggests that a post-operative patient who is asymptomatic with a haemoglobin of 90g/L probably does not require a transfusion. As mentioned earlier, a transfusion was often ordered in the past simply because a physician considered it a good thing to do, and that it would probably do the patient some good. This would be fine but for a number of problems, such as:

• In practice, whilst the ABO/Rh systems are the most important, there are a host of other blood group antigens (with names such as Duffy and Kell) that can generate antibodies. The more transfused a person becomes, the greater the likelihood that these antibodies will build up to become a real clinical and laboratory issue.

• We are biologically programmed to collect and save iron in stores all over the body. People who are hyper-transfused often have problems in various organs, as the build-up of this iron can cause damage to the tissues (haemosiderosis). Since a single unit of blood contains some 250mg of iron, 15 units can more than double the body's iron stores.

• Transfused blood may contain pathogenic organisms (such as viruses, bacteria and parasites), although, fortunately, due to screening, this is becoming less of a problem. Infection can also occur via the site of the infusion.

For several reasons, not simply because of the above, the present view is that transfusion should be reserved only for those patients who are in danger of losing their lives, or those who will show a measurable improvement that is not achievable by other means. The cautionary tale mentioned earlier, about the woman with sickle cell disease (see page 14), underlines this point. It follows that the requirement for a transfusion can only be made clinically, not in the laboratory. However much experience is available within the blood bank, and clinical advice should always be sought if cases fall outside established practice or guidelines.

Indications for blood transfusion

A transfusion should *not* be ordered simply because a patient's haemoglobin is less than a certain number. Reasons for ordering a transfusion can be many and varied, but major life-threatening indications include:

- Chronic and serious anaemia that is refractive to other treatment, e.g. severe cases of the haemoglobinopathies (sickle cell disease or thalassaemia)
- Life-threatening emergencies, e.g. rupture of an aortic abdominal aneurysm, or massive blood loss after a road traffic accident or after surgery
- Haemorrhage, e.g. in haemophilia, or overdoses of anticoagulants (such as warfarin or heparin) or anti-platelet agents (such as aspirin or clopidogrel) or thrombocytopenia.

Indications for blood products

All hospitals need to deal with haemorrhage due to causes such as prolonged PT, PTT, decreased fibrinogen, over-anticoagulation with warfarin or heparin, trauma, surgery or disseminated intravascular coagulation.

As discussed earlier, the blood bank can provide not only red blood cells, but also platelets and coagulation proteins such as fibrinogen, Factor VII and Factor VIII that we met in Chapter 3. Other components are fresh frozen plasma (FFP) and cryoprecipitate. These will be needed by people at risk of haemorrhage, or with actual haemorrhagic blood loss, but who do not need red blood cells, such as those with haemophilia and severe von Willebrand's disease.

As fragments of cells, platelets will also need to be checked for blood group compatibility. Platelets cannot be frozen, so have to be fresh, or at least stored at 4°C, and are often given for life-threatening thrombocytopenia. Albumin (generally as a 20% preparation) is also available for people with low levels or who have had heavy burns (although only regional centres will deal with these risky patients) or ascites.

When things go wrong

No human activity is free of the risk of possible error, and blood transfusion is no exception. An incompatible transfusion can kill. But how can it happen? Errors can and do occur at all places in the 'journey' the blood takes from donor to recipient. However, it is generally recognised that most errors happen in the laboratory and/or once the blood has left the blood bank for its destination.

Laboratory error

Clearly, the packs of blood arrive from the NHS Blood and Transplant Service (NHSBTS, formerly the National Blood Transfusion Service) in good shape, typed for ABO and Rh groups, and also screened for major infective agents such as the viruses that cause hepatitis and HIV. However, the blood sample from the recipient may be labelled incorrectly. The next source of error may be the incorrect labelling of the same portion of each potential donor pack. Next, there could be an error in the Cross-match itself. These are rare because the lab has usually invested heavily in the technology and reagents to ensure that, if an adverse reaction is happening, it is detected. However, if the Cross-match goes wrong, which is a false negative, a possibly incompatible unit of blood may be issued. If several packs are identified, the lab may assign an incompatible unit to the patient.

Post-laboratory error

These errors inevitably involve the wrong blood being given to the wrong patient. The wrong pack of blood may be collected from the issuing refrigerator at the blood bank, or the blood may be given in error to the wrong patient. A common source of confusion is that two or more patients are due to be transfused at the same place, at the same time.

Many of these errors are simply cases of incorrect patient identification, generally by a misunderstood verbal recognition question, or by misreading the patient's ID strip on their wrist.

What do we do about errors?

Early reactions

In an acute setting, how do you know there is a problem? Remember of course that patients may not recognise there is a problem (especially if they are unconscious!). But what should a practitioner look for? The symptoms and signs of a transfusion reaction vary enormously (see Table 5).

Table 5: Symptoms and signs of a potential transfusion incompatibility

Symptoms	Signs
Cough and/or headache Flushing/rash Anxiety/agitation Chills Nausea and vomiting Trembles/shakes Shortness of breath, chest pain	Fever (temp spike >40°C) Hypotension Oozing from wounds Haemoglobinuria Tachycardia (>100 bpm)

However, there can also be acute non-red blood cell reactions. For example, acute urticarial reactions (such as hives) and anaphylaxis may be the result of the recipient responding to the donor's plasma proteins. If so, antihistamines are one possible treatment.

If a reaction is suspected, the infusion should be stopped immediately. All good hospitals will have a defined protocol that must be followed. Clearly, clinical treatment will depend on the severity of the reaction, which, if it's not too bad, can be rapidly reversed. But severe reactions can be life-threatening and will be treated accordingly (e.g. with rapid admission to the ICU if there is disseminated intravascular coagulation, with ventilation, adrenaline, hydrocortisone).

One 'mechanical' way of treating an acute reaction is to try to 'flush' it out. This is attempted by giving fluids, but clearly requires good renal function. If there is massive donor red blood cell destruction, there may well be hyperkalaemia (high potassium). Possible treatment options would be to:

- Insert a urinary catheter to monitor urine output
- Give fluids (IV colloids) to maintain urine output >1.5ml/kg/hour
- If urine output <1.5ml/kg/h, insert CVP line and give fluid challenge
- If urine output <1.5ml/kg/h and CVP adequate, give frusemide 80–120mg
- If urine output still <1.5ml/kg/h, consult senior staff for advice

The donor blood pack will be collected by the lab staff, and a blood sample will be taken from the patient. Both will be thoroughly (re)analysed. Most are subsequently found to be ABO incompatibilities – Rhesus problems are less common.

Late reactions

Problems at 12/24 hours to 3 days may involve major organs such as acute renal failure (with or without haematuria or haemoglobinuria), jaundice, congestive heart failure due to circulatory overload, and pulmonary oedema with or without adult respiratory distress syndrome.

Febrile reactions (generally with a slow-rising temperature, peaking at over 40°C) are seen in 0.5–1% of transfusions and these may be due to anti-HLA reactions. Later complications (3–14 days) after an incompatible transfusion may consist of a 'new' immunological reaction by the recipient to the donor red blood cells, causing the destruction of the latter. This time period may also see transfusion-related infections that have escaped the screening process. There may also be reactions with rare antigens too weak to be detected in the laboratory.

Post-transfusion purpura is characterised by a severe thrombocytopenia (which can last from 2 weeks to 2 months) and is caused by antibodies to antigens on the surface of platelets. In the short term, a thrombocytopenia may develop in the hypertransfused patient, as infused blood is generally platelet-free. If the patient is haemorrhaging, platelet transfusion may be required.

Repercussions

There will of course be an 'inquest', the findings of which will strengthen the system and so minimise the possibility of a similar error recurring. A report will be forwarded to the relevant authorities (such as the National Patient Safety Agency) and also to the Serious Hazard of Transfusion (SHOT) group. The 2005 SHOT report makes essential reading (see the SHOT website, page 49). Of 609 reported cases, 485 were incorrect blood component transfused. However, a staggering 481 (>99%) were classified as being 'no-harm', in which the patient suffered minor (or not minor) morbidity. These 485 may be classified as follows:

- Failure to provide blood of appropriate specification or that did not meet the patient's special requirements   n=141 (29%)

- 'Wrong blood' events, where a patient received a blood component intended for a different patient or of an incorrect group   n=87 (18%)

- Events relating to administration of anti-D immunoglobulin   n=87 (18%)

- 'Unsafe' transfusion, where there were handling or storage errors   n=79 (16%)

- Inappropriate or unnecessary transfusions   n=67 (14%)

- Other pre-transfusion testing errors – including incorrect D groups, missed antigens and missed serological incompatibility   n=24 (5%)

Prevention

Naturally, there are many steps designed to prevent a transfusion error: generally, check, check and check again. Laser bar coding is being introduced so that the sample can be traced from the requesting blood sample all the way back to the patient.

Many hospitals have a policy whereby at least two members of staff check the blood they are about to transfuse into each one of their patients. This approach has been proven to reduce mistakes and serious hazards involving transfusion. Indeed, SHOT itself reports that ABO incompatible transfusions have shown a 54% reduction since 2001/2002. Curiously, SHOT notes that there has been a reduction in transfusion-related acute lung injury since only male donors have been used for FFP and plasma in platelet concentrates. Blood transfusions outside core hours are less safe – and so it is a SHOT recommendation that these are kept to a minimum, and extra vigilance maintained.

Many wards and hospitals have their own formal policy, and professional bodies (such as the Royal College of Nursing, Institute of Biomedical Sciences, and the British Committee for Standards in Haematology) also offer guidelines.

Recommended websites

www.bcshguidelines.com/4_haematology_guidelines.html

www.nrls.npsa.nhs.uk/resources/

www.blood.co.uk/

www.learnbloodtransfusion.org.uk

www.nhs.uk/conditions/Blood-transfusion/Pages/Introduction.aspx

www.shotuk.org/

Summary

- Blood transfusion is a therapy generally reserved for urgent and life-threatening clinical situations such as blood loss. It is now rarely seen as a temporary 'cure' for anaemia, where an alternative such as iron may be preferable.
- Blood groups are A, B, AB and O, but Rh D is also important.
- Requests are usually to 'Group and Save', and to 'Cross-match'
- The blood bank also provides platelets, albumin and coagulation factors.
- Incompatible blood transfusion can be fatal and will lead to symptoms such as rash, shortness of breath, headache and cough.
- Most incompatible reactions are due to clerical and/or identification errors.

5

Immunology

Key words:
Autoantibodies

Anti-nuclear antibodies

Rheumatoid factor

Key pathological expressions:
Autoimmunity

Rheumatoid arthritis

Immunodeficiency

Hypersensitivity

An explanation of terms:

Chapter 2 (on white blood cells) has already introduced key concepts of immunology and inflammation, and the importance of lymphocytes, neutrophils and antibodies. Most of the clinical aspects of immunology can be summarised as follows:

- Autoimmunity is where the body attacks itself.
- Immunodeficiency is where the immune system is unable to adequately defend the body from micropathogens.
- Hypersensitivity is where the immune system responds too vigorously to a relatively innocuous stimulus.

Autoimmunity

A key concept in immunology is the immune system's ability to recognise its own cells and tissues as being 'self'. Anything that is 'non-self' is therefore expected to be foreign (viruses and bacteria), and potentially pathogenic, so it must be destroyed, which is all well and good. The trouble begins when the immune system mistakenly considers its own tissues to be 'non-self', and so starts an attack. This process is autoimmunity.

Autoimmune diseases account for a considerable percentage of human morbidity and mortality. Table 6 (below) lists some of the cells and organs that may be subject to this type of attack, and the clinical condition that follows in each case. A major pathological finding in each autoimmune disease is the presence of a defined autoantibody (directed towards the organ or cell in question) that actually does the damage. Consequently, the presence of the disease is often ultimately defined by the laboratory's ability to find and report this autoantibody.

Table 6: Some cells and organs subject to autoimmune attack

Cells/organ attacked	Clinical consequence
Thyroid tissue	Thyroiditis
Red blood cells	Autoimmune haemolytic anaemia
Joints	Rheumatoid arthritis
The pancreas	Diabetes
The kidney	Glomerulonephritis
Parts of the stomach	Pernicious anaemia

Connective tissue disease

The most common autoimmune diseases are undoubtedly of musculoskeletal tissue. This group includes conditions such as rheumatoid arthritis (RA) and systemic lupus erythematosus (SLE). The common degenerative bone and joint disease osteoarthritis is not autoimmune. There are no specific routine haematology or biochemistry blood tests for these conditions although there may well be an abnormal white blood cell count, erythrocyte sedimentation rate (ESR) and C-reactive protein (CRP). The other major tests are:

- Rheumatoid factor: This is an autoantibody to an immunoglobulin, and is present in about 80% of those with rheumatoid arthritis. It follows that about 20% of people with rheumatoid arthritis have 'sero-negative' disease.
- Antinuclear antibodies: These are present in many people with systemic lupus erythematosus (SLE) or scleroderma.
- A well-equipped department will be able to do tests on white blood cells, possibly with a machine called a flow cytometer. However, such a machine may also be housed in a haematology unit, where it may be used to examine leukaemic cells.

As usual, the laboratory provides guidance on diagnosis and the effects of treatment. As many of these diseases are inflammatory, it is hoped that particular treatments (such as immunosuppression) will improve laboratory markers of inflammation such as CRP. In this respect, the ESR may be used as a simple marker of the effects of steroids in certain connective tissue diseases such as temporal arteritis. The daily dose of steroid can therefore be titrated up or down as laboratory tests (as so, we assume, the disease process) are influenced.

Polymyositis and dermatomyositis are inflammatory diseases of muscle and/or skin, and where there is damage to muscle, there is also likely to be raised creatine kinase. However, this enzyme is also raised in damage to the muscles of the heart, and is likely to occur after a myocardial infarction (see Chapter 9, page 91).

Organ-specific autoimmune disease

As is shown in Table 6 (page 52), other autoimmune diseases (such as of the thyroid) attack precise organs. All are characterised by an autoantibody to that particular tissue, which can be demonstrated in the laboratory. There is often a family link in autoimmunity, so other family members may be at risk of an autoimmune disease if one is diagnosed in a close relative. In addition, many people with an autoantibody to one tissue may also have an autoantibody to a different tissue. Irritatingly, there are few laboratory tests that are sensitive and specific enough to allow a firm and unequivocal diagnosis.

Immunodeficiency

Deprived of a functioning immune system, the individual is open to attack by micropathogens. This is inevitably due to the inability to make antibodies, and the consequent inability of the white cells to digest bacteria. Aetiology is generally genetic/congenital, or secondary. The former will be evident in the neonate, whilst the latter will be caused by an external agent, and generally in the adult. As the bone marrow is where white cells (and therefore the ability to make antibodies) are produced, stress or damage to this organ, perhaps by cytotoxic chemotherapy or cancer, is a leading cause of immunodeficiency. An established alternative cause of secondary deficiency is infection with HIV.

The laboratory demonstration of immunodeficiency is with reduced levels, or the absence, of antibodies. The laboratory can also show when white blood cells themselves are dysfunctional – one of the most common such diseases being chronic granulomatous disease.

Hypersensitivity

Most of us produce a measured and appropriate response to a micropathogen. However, in some people, the response far exceeds that which is actually needed. This leads to hypersensitivity, a condition said to be present in 10% of the population. The factor causing the over-reaction is called an allergen, which causes an allergy. Common allergens include:

- foodstuffs such as peanuts, pecans, pine nuts, walnuts, shellfish, egg albumin, wheat, maize, kiwifruit, milk, soy and chestnut
- invertebrate material: such as house dust mites and storage mites (integument and faeces)
- plant material such as pollen (typically ragweed), poison ivy and certain oaks
- drugs such as antibiotics, muscle relaxants, painkillers, aspirin and non-steroidal anti-inflammatory drugs
- venoms such as insect bites and stings.

Clinical allergy

Interaction of the allergens listed above with a type of antibody (IgE) on the surface of certain white cells (basophils) causes the release of a host of small molecules that cause a wide variety of symptoms. These include:

- asthma, which may cause problems with breathing, tightness of the chest, cough and wheezing
- allergic conjunctivitis, which is similar to rhinitis, but inflames the conjunctiva (rather than the nasal lining), with the same pain, irritation and itching, and with tears
- eczema, which is an umbrella term for several skin conditions that include rash, swelling, dryness and itching
- intestinal problems, typically pain and cramps, which are probably due to the action of histamine by white cells of the intestines
- rhinitis, meaning inflammation of the nose, but also of the soft tissues of the nasal passage, with itching, blockage and a mucinous discharge
- urticaria, also known as hives, which is a raised rash (weal) most often found on the arms, legs and back, whilst facial urticaria is common with food allergies.

Several of these symptoms can be present concurrently. For example, the most common manifestation of hypersensitivity is hay fever, which is likely to involve a mixture of rhinitis, conjunctivitis and often some pulmonary symptoms such as asthma.

The laboratory

The Immunology Laboratory will test for overall levels of IgE, but also allergen-specific IgE. This testing (also described as product-resolved diagnosis) can identify IgE that is reactive towards certain grasses, fruit, egg and nuts. Antibodies may also be present in farmer's lung, allergic alveolitis and pigeon fancier's lung.

Treatment

This depends on the stimulus. Generally, an antihistamine such as piriton is used to block the histamine receptor. Other treatments (such as sodium cromoglicate) stabilise the basophil membrane and so suppress degranulation. A variety of agents can be delivered by aerosol directly to the lung in cases of asthma. The agents in these inhalers include salbutamol (a beta$_2$ adrenoreceptor agonist) and other adrenaline agonists (such as epinephrine). For severe disease, glucocorticosteroids are preferred for long-term control.

Recommended websites

www.allergyuk.org

www.arthritisresearchuk.org/arthritis.../rheumatoid-arthritis.aspx

www.immunology.org

www.nras.org.uk (National Rheumatoid Arthritis Society)

www.rheumatology.org/practice/clinical/classification/index.asp

Summary

- The leading class of immunological disease is autoimmunity, which in turn is principally found in rheumatoid arthritis and SLE. These diseases are characterised by autoantibodies such as rheumatoid factor and antinuclear antibodies.
- Immunodeficiency is present when the body is unable to defend itself from micropathogens. It may be due to damage to the bone marrow or the effects of the human immunodeficiency virus (HIV).
- Hypersensitivity is present when the body over-reacts to a stimulus (an allergen), causing conditions involving allergic reactions such as asthma, conjunctivitis and skin rash.

Case study 4

An 80-year-old man, with a body mass index of 34.8kg/m^2, complains to his GP that he has had worsening pains in both knees for six months, the pain in the right being markedly greater than that in the left. The pain is minimal upon rising in the morning, but gets worse during the day. The patient is sent for X-rays, a full blood count, ESR, CRP and rheumatoid factor.

The full blood count is entirely normal, but the ESR is very slightly increased at 14mm/hour (reference range <10mm/hour). The rheumatoid factor is negative (result 1/20, reference titre <1/40), as is the CRP at <5g/L (reference range <5g/L). The X-ray points to moderate erosions in the right knee and mild erosions in the left, which is consistent with the history of pain.

Interpretation

The only abnormality is the very marginally increased ESR. The rheumatoid factor titre is well within the reference range. The history points to a chronic connective tissues disease such as osteoarthritis (OA) or rheumatoid arthritis (RA). The rheumatoid factor within the reference range does not exclude the latter (the RA may be sero-negative), but the lack of any gross abnormalities points to the former. Excess weight is the major risk factor for OA – in this case there is marked obesity. If the patient had RA, the presentation would be different, with several sets of swollen and painful joints, and perhaps other factors such as early morning stiffness and more abnormalities in the blood analysis.

Notably, there is minimal pain after a night's rest, but the pain increases during the day, probably as the damaged joints are used more. This is more a feature of OA: in RA the pain is present upon rising and is often consistent throughout the day, but this is often because those with RA have learned to manage their pain by resting as much as possible. The normal CRP counts against an overt inflammatory condition. Initial treatment is analgesia with strong advice to lose weight, especially as overweight is a major risk factor for diabetes. Surgery (joint replacement) may be required if the patient is sufficiently fit.

Part 2

Biochemistry

Objectives and scope

Biochemistry shares many similarities with haematology and immunology. Indeed, alongside blood transfusion, they are often described together as 'blood science'. There are also numerous instances where the pathophysiology of one spills over to influence the other – and renal disease is an excellent example of this, as we shall see.

As for haematology, it is taken as understood that all blood tubes and forms must be fully labelled by those taking the blood in order to minimise the risk of (possibly fatal) error. Indeed, the laboratory will be within its right to decline to test a particular sample that is incorrectly or inadequately labelled.

The major difference between these two sciences is that almost all biochemistry is done on serum obtained from clotted blood, although blood glucose is the prime example of a biochemistry test done on blood that has to be anticoagulated. Thus testing can only be performed on blood that is collected in the correct tube. Failure to do so will, at best, result in a polite phone call from the lab explaining the problem and its remedy. At worst, a report will be returned a day or so later with a comment such as 'inappropriate blood sample received, please repeat'. Fortunately, many blood tubes have different-coloured tops to help this process and minimise errors. Therefore, again, if in doubt, PHONE.

A note on units

As for haematology, here is a note on units. Few of us with an interest in lipids will disagree that a total cholesterol result of 8.5 is undesirable, even though the correct terms are 8.5mmol/L. However, this will certainly be a problem to those (such as Americans) reporting cholesterol in different units of mg/dL. For example, their result would be 325! It matters not so much that the correct unit of, shall we say, serum calcium is given (for example, as 4.5mmol/L, or in shorthand simply as 4.5) but it does matter that this particular result is very serious and demands immediate attention.

Biochemistry Report Form

As for haematology, this form (reporting the author's blood) was produced by the author's hospital laboratory. Once more, the report offers (from left to right) a column of words and abbreviations (particular tests), a column of numbers (the results), another column of numbers and letters (units), and yet another column of numbers (the normal or target range). Again, the main objective of this section of the book is to explain what all this means.

CLINICAL CHEMISTRY City Hospital NHS Trust Birmingham B18 7QH

Surname	BLANN	Address		Unit No.	ZC01282337	ASCOT CLINIC (CHEM)
Forename	ANDREW					
D.O.B.	11.08.54				Not given	
				NHS No.		

Ethnic group: White – Any other   **Clinical Details**   Lab No. C,01.0025121.G

Urea	4.1	mmol/1	(3.0–8.3)
Sodium	142	mmol/1	(133–144)
Potassiium	3.8	mmol/1	(3.4–5.1)
Creatinine	89	umol/1	(44–133)
Total Protein	65	g/l	(63–84)
Albumin	36	g/l	(35–50)
Bilirubin	7	umol/1	(5–17)
Alk Phosphatase	56	g/l	(20–130)
Alanine A.T.	38	g/l	(<50)
Cholesterol	3.7	mmol/1	(3.1–6.5)
Triglycerides	1.25	mmol/1	(0.85–1.98)
HDL-Cholesterol	1.2	mmol/1	(1.2–1.7)

Tests: CRE, HDL, LFT, LIP, UE	Check Clinician	Date received	**09.02.01**
		Date reported	**12.02.01**

Figure 6: Biochemistry Report Form

Learning objectives – Biochemistry

Having completed this section, you will:

1. Appreciate that almost all biochemistry tests need to be done on serum. The principal exception is glucose.

2. Recognise the major areas of interest:
   - Fluid and electrolytes balance
   - Sodium and potassium
   - The kidney
   - Liver function tests and plasma proteins
   - Atherosclerosis and its risk factors (e.g. diabetes)
   - Calcium and bone
   - Thyroid function

3. Describe major clinical problems associated with each of these areas, such as:
   - Dehydration
   - Renal and liver failure
   - Diabetic ketoacidosis

4. Interpret simple biochemistry results, such as:
   - A urea of 21.4 with a creatinine of 145
   - A bilirubin of 7 with an alkaline phosphatase of 890
   - A calcium of 1.9 with an albumin of 32

5. Understand the basic purpose of a Biochemistry Laboratory

6

Water, urea and electrolytes

Key words:
Sodium
Potassium

Key pathological expressions:
Hypernatraemia
Hyponatraemia
Hyperkalaemia
Hypokalaemia
Dehydration
Oedema

An explanation of terms:
Urea and electrolytes (U&Es) are undoubtedly the most commonly requested biochemistry tests. Urea is the major excretory product of our biochemical metabolism, whilst creatinine is a more specialised product of the breakdown of proteins. An explanation of the role of urea and creatinine is best left for the section on renal disease that follows.

Electrolytes are charged atoms (ions) or molecules that are involved in the passage of electricity. They are often written with a small plus or minus (like Na^+ and Cl^-), indicating their electrical charge, although, in practice, charge is often ignored. Sodium (Na), hydrogen (H) and potassium (K) are most commonly requested whilst others, such as Cl (chloride) and HCO_3 (bicarbonate), are less frequently requested, although the latter can be important, especially in acidosis, as discussed in Chapter 12. It can also be argued that calcium (Ca) is an electrolyte, but it belongs in a section of its own (Chapter 10). However, before we embark on a discussion of U&Es, we must consider water.

Water

A curious place to begin, you may think, but water is fundamental to all blood tests, as the concentration [C] of any substance is given by the mass (amount) [M] of that substance, divided by the volume [V] of the fluid it is dissolved in (i.e. water in blood). In the clinical setting, however, the total mass and total volume of fluids are the differences between 'in' (eating and drinking – M_{in} and V_{in}) and 'out' (excreting – M_{out} as faeces and V_{out} as urine). This leads to the equation:

$$\text{Concentration} = \frac{\text{Mass}_{in} - \text{Mass}_{out}}{\text{Volume}_{in} - \text{Volume}_{out}}$$

This means that the concentration of something is a balance, and the concentration will be higher if there is more of it in a fixed volume, or if there is the same amount of it in a smaller volume. We must therefore consider the state of hydration or dehydration of our patients. As we shall see, the amount of water in the blood is regulated by the kidney, so problems with this organ can lead to water retention (and thus, possibly, oedema), or excess water loss (V_{out}), as too much urine is made (diuresis, leading to dehydration). Water loss as excess urine is clear, but it is not so easy to account for water loss via sweat, through the lungs (especially on hot days), and in faeces (especially in diarrhoea). These small and separate (by themselves) losses of water can add up to a considerable amount.

Sodium

This is the primary electrolyte in the blood, as there is more of it than any other. Faced with increases or decreases, we need to consider the equation, concentration = mass/volume.

One good explanation for changes in serum sodium is that the diet is abnormally rich or low in this salt. Another reason is that the amount of water in the blood has increased or fallen. Since the kidney regulates both these aspects, changes in sodium may indicate problems with this organ.

Hypernatraemia may be due to a salt-rich diet (e.g. high M_{in}) and/or a degree of dehydration – the classical clinical sign of which is loss of elasticity of the skin (the pinch test – although this is unreliable in the elderly). However, the most common reason is water loss, possibly due to insufficient intake in drinking (i.e. low V_{in}), excess loss in urine, or losses in sweat and diarrhoea (i.e. high V_{out}). Clinically, the simplest treatment is to replace fluid orally, if possible. If this is not possible (maybe because the patient is in a coma) then water can be infused as part of a dextrose drip.

Similarly, **hyponatraemia** may be due to retention of water (low V_{out}) and/or excessive loss of sodium (high M_{out}). For this most common in-hospital electrolyte disturbance (15% of patients), very rare causes include insufficient sodium in the diet, and very high levels of proteins or lipids in the blood. A recognised sign of this fluid retention is oedema, although this may not always be present.

The most common sign of oedema is swollen ankles, and is relatively easy to spot. However, excess fluid in the lungs, causing pulmonary oedema, is far harder to diagnose and is clinically more dangerous. Oedema is also associated with heart failure and hypoalbuminaemia. In some cases, water retention can be treated with thiazide drugs, but this can be dangerous if the kidneys are not functioning adequately.

Potassium

Many aspects of potassium regulation are similar to sodium (such as intake and outlet), but with a number of crucial differences. The first is that the majority of our potassium is within cells, not in the plasma – the reverse of sodium. The second is the relationship between potassium and hydrogen ions: as hydrogen ions increase (as in acidosis), potassium is displaced from the cell and enters the plasma. The reverse is true in alkalosis. Overall, potassium (unlike sodium) does not vary a great deal in response to big changes in water balance.

Hyperkalaemia may be due to renal problems (such as failure to excrete sufficient potassium), acidosis, or release from damaged cells (such as destruction of red blood cells, or tumour cells by chemotherapy, or crush injuries). However, whatever the reason, it may be serious as high levels (for example, >7mmol/L) can contribute to cardiac arrest because of interference with nerves. Indeed…

> ## High serum potassium kills people!

Therefore high potassium is the most common and most serious electrolyte emergency, and treatment includes insulin and glucose to get potassium into cells. Other treatments include calcium gluconate, resonium A and dialysis.

Causes of **hypokalaemia** (serum potassium <3.3mmol/L) include the reverse of the above, such as alkalosis, in addition to loss of potassium in diarrhoea and vomiting, from the kidney, or inappropriate use of corticosteroids or thiazide drugs. In the case of the latter, a reactive alkalosis may result. Treatment focuses on replacement, such as oral salts, or a potassium-rich drip supplement.

Intravenous (IV) fluids

It follows from much of the above that loss of fluid balance is important, and can be restored by IV fluids, usually in 500ml- or 1 litre- bags. Water cannot be given by itself, as it will destroy red blood cells, so must be given as 5% dextrose. Saline (0.9% NaCl) rehydrates plasma and lymph, but not cells, whilst plasma expanders replace fluid deficits in the blood alone. Most clinical situations can be managed with these fluids, plus 1.26% bicarbonate (to treat acidosis) and concentrated supplements (such as potassium). However, misuse of IV fluids can, of course, cause the reverse of what is being treated, so monitoring is crucial.

Laboratory monitoring is by frequent measurement of serum electrolytes, but clinical assessment (such as pulse, blood pressure, body weight) can also be important. Measurement of fluids taken orally (by drinking) and the volume of urine produced is important, but these will not always add up to 100%, due to 'insensible' losses that are not easy to calculate (from sweat, lungs, and in faeces). Also, if someone is vomiting, this will compound a possible state of dehydration.

Summary

- Overall, U&Es are often used to monitor renal function.
- Consider the equation: concentration = mass/volume.
- Hypernatraemia may be due to decreased water intake, increased sodium intake, or decreased sodium intake with greater decrease in water intake. Rarely, it may be due to renal disease with impaired ability to excrete sodium.
- Hyponatraemia may be due to fluid retention or insufficient sodium, possibly resulting from a poor diet or excess excretion.
- Hyperkalaemia can follow from renal failure, acidosis or damaged cells, and can be life-threatening.
- Hypokalaemia may also follow renal disease, but can also result from gastrointestinal losses, alkalosis and misuse of drugs such as thiazides.
- Fluids can be rapidly replaced by IV infusion, but must be adequately monitored and attention paid to renal functioning.

7

Investigation of renal function

Key words:

Urea
Glomerular filtration rate (GFR)
Creatinine
Uric acid/urate

Key pathological expressions:

Acute renal injury
Chronic kidney disease
Nephrotic syndrome
Glomerulonephritis

An explanation of terms:

Whilst the heart, brain and lungs are the primary concern in emergency care, the kidney is certainly the next organ in importance. This organ consists of millions of single functional units, called nephrons (hence nephrology and nephropathy).

Kidney functions

The functions of the kidney can be summarised as follows:

- Homeostasis: Regulating the volume of blood by making urine (diuresis), in maintaining the acid/base balance (i.e., the pH, as may be assessed with hydrogen ions and bicarbonate ions), and in correcting the levels of electrolytes (sodium and potassium)
- Endocrine responsiveness and activity: Regulating blood pressure via local hormones, influencing the bone marrow in the production of red blood cells, and contributing to the level of serum calcium
- Excreting our metabolic waste products, principally the nitrogen-rich molecules urea, uric acid and creatinine

The top part of the mini-organ of the nephron is the glomerulus – the part that interfaces directly with the blood. It is an important filter: most of the good things in blood pass directly through it, and are later re-absorbed in the tubes and loop of Henle. Meanwhile, the unwanted leftovers make up the urine. Hence we are interested in how well this small area of the nephron functions.

Tests of glomerular function

As mentioned earlier, kidney disease is frequently accompanied by changes in U&Es, but especially in serum creatinine and urea. If the former slowly rises up to 150μmol/L and beyond to, shall we say, 180, then renal function is deteriorating and the patient is increasingly in need of a referral to a renal physician. Creatinine itself has few physiological effects – it is most useful as a marker of renal function. However, rising urea is dangerous, as it can adversely influence the function of red blood cells and other cells. Levels may also rise because of a decrease in effective circulating blood.

An alternative test of the integrity of this organ is protein in the urine (proteinuria), which can be determined by dipsticks. We all lose a small amount of protein in this way (generally <30mg in a 24-hour period), and this is physiologically acceptable. Nonetheless, if this loss becomes considerable then renal function must be deteriorating.

However, the ultimate test of kidney function is the rate at which blood is filtered by passing over the glomerulus to produce an early form of urine, i.e. the glomerular filtration rate (GFR). Ideally, this would be over 90ml/minute/$1.73m^2$, but it is accepted that it falls slowly with age.

Historically, the GFR was calculated by calculating the product of the urine creatinine concentration and 24-hour urine, and then dividing this figure by the concentration of creatinine in the serum. This was also known as the creatinine clearance test. Unfortunately, this process was seriously prone to error, and is rarely used any more.

Instead, the GFR is now determined by an equation that requires only serum creatinine, sex and age, and also either weight or whether the person is of African ancestry (see Recommended websites, page 73). The Cockcroft-Gault equation calls for serum creatinine, weight, age and sex, whilst the MDRD formula requires age, sex, creatinine and race. There are free online calculators for these methods, but the practitioner must check with the local Pathology Laboratory to determine which to use.

Generally, as the creatinine rises, the GFR falls. At the clinical level, the GFR can fall considerably (for example, to 15–20% of normal), and the serum creatinine can rise appreciably, before the patient becomes symptomatic.

Renal disease

The most common causes of kidney problems can be divided into three types (see Figure 7):

• Pre-renal disease is characterised by factors such as insufficient blood entering the kidney, which may be due to occlusive renal artery stenosis, abdominal aortic aneurysm, or poor cardiac output as may be present in heart failure.

• True renal disease is often seen in septic shock, glomerulonephritis (i.e. inflammation of the kidney), in the presence of toxins or amyloid, renal carcinoma (or secondary metastases), and in physical damage with blood loss. This state of the disease may be called acute tubular necrosis.

• Post-renal disease is present if there are problems downstream of the kidney, such as with the ureter, the bladder or the urethra. Most common causes of this are kidney stones, carcinoma of the bladder or prostate, benign prostatic hyperplasia, or infections. All these limit or prevent urine from flowing out, so that it eventually backs up to the kidneys themselves.

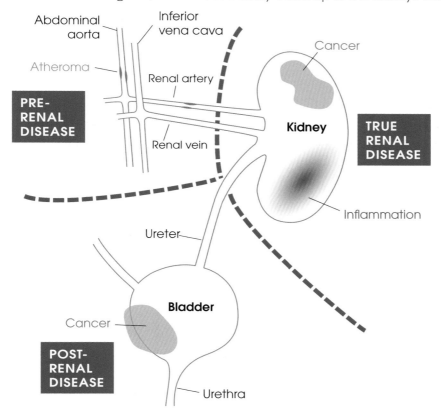

Figure 7: Aetiology of renal disease

Thus in both pre- and post-renal disease, there is nothing intrinsically wrong with the tissues of the kidney itself, or its functioning: the problem is with the tubes at either end. However, failure to correct pre- or post-renal disease will inevitably lead to true renal disease. Management of renal disease depends on the particular aetiology and thus the correction of pre-/post-renal factors, if appropriate. This may be, for example, antibiotics and immunosuppression for glomerulonephritis, angioplasty for renal artery stenosis, or surgery for bladder carcinoma.

Biochemical monitoring will be by U&Es, and clinically by urine production. If the potassium rises dangerously, dialysis may well be called for. Recovery from acute renal injury may be accompanied by a marked diuresis, with a massive increase in urine production (possibly as much as 7 litres a day!), so that fluid balance may need to be checked. Soon after, a return to normal diuresis can be expected.

Acute renal injury (ARI)

This may be defined by the ratio of the relative rise in urea being greater than the relative rise in creatinine, not simply the levels themselves. Other biochemical abnormalities include acidosis (because the kidney can no longer excrete hydrogen ions) and hyperkalaemia. Of course, the patient is likely to be able to help in describing any changes in making urine. A likely story is of a sudden fall-off, or even cessation, in diuresis.

However, if the damage to the kidney in ARI is excessive, and leads to destruction of the nephron, it may well become permanently and irreversibly dysfunctional, in which case there will be deterioration to chronic kidney disease.

Chronic kidney disease (CKD)

CKD is the progressive and (invariably) irreversible destruction of kidney tissues, and is typically noted when the GFR falls in stages below <60 ml/minute (Table 7). Using U&Es, CKD can be plotted by the relative rise in urea, compared to the rise in creatinine. However, unlike ARI, in CKD there is a greater increase in creatinine and a more modest rise in urea.

The consequences of CKD are not unlike those of ARI, principally with disturbances in sodium, hydrogen and water metabolism – there may be fluid overload (with oedema) or fluid depletion (with dehydration). If present, a metabolic acidosis will be evident with a low level of bicarbonate, and this may also contribute to hyperkalaemia. However, this may independently arise from the individual's increasingly impaired ability to excrete potassium, and may be life-threatening. Low levels of calcium, and hence raised parathyroid hormone

(PTH), may be present, as the kidney loses its ability to promote calcium absorption in the intestines. Similarly, anaemia is likely to result, as the impaired kidney will no longer be making erythropoietin, a growth factor required by those bone marrow stem cells that are responsible for red blood cell production.

Clinical features of CKD also include nocturia (resulting from uneven diuresis) and hypertension. Good management will address sodium and water intake, and diuretics may be necessary (depending on the degree of renal (dys)function). Hyperkalaemia may be managed with Resonium A and a low-protein diet may help in minimising nitrogen, and thus the need to excrete it as urea and creatinine.

Table 7: Stages of CKD

Stage	eGFR	Description and management
I	>90	Normal renal function. Treatment should control whatever cardiovascular risk factors are present.
II	60–89	Mildly reduced renal function. This stage should not be diagnosed on eGFR alone but urinalysis, structural abnormalities or genetic factors may be considered. Observe and control cardiovascular risk factors.
IIIa	45–59	Moderate decrease in renal function, with or without other evidence of kidney damage. More stringent control of cardiovascular risk factor. Consider low-dose statin regardless of serum cholesterol, and an ACEI/ARB regardless of blood pressure, target <140/90.
IIIb	30–44	Marked decrease in renal function, with or without other evidence of kidney damage. Statin and ACEI/ARB likely to be advisable. Check haemoglobin to identify anaemia. Blood pressure target <135/85.
IV	15–29	Severely reduced renal function. Prophylactic pharmacotherapy mandatory. Measure calcium, phosphate and PTH. Plan for end-stage renal disease.
V	<15	Very severe (end-stage) renal failure. Preparation for dialysis or transplant.

ACEI = angiotensin converting enzyme inhibitor   ARB = angiotensin receptor blocker
PTH = parathyroid hormone
Note: Blood pressure targets are lower in cardiovascular disease, SLE and diabetes.

Management of renal disease

Wherever possible, the cause of the disease must be identified and addressed (see Figure 7). ARI must be treated urgently, and is reversible, with treatment depending aetiology (such as immunosuppression for inflammation). Although CKD is essentially irreversible, its advance can be retarded by treatment of risk factors such as high blood pressure (see Table 7 page 71). Those with proteinuria, diabetes and microalbuminuria need to maintain their systolic blood pressure safely within a target range of 120–129mmHg and their diastolic blood pressure below 80mmHg.

The National Institute for Health and Clinical Excellence (NICE) provides guidance on the management of CKD, through Clinical Guideline (CG) 73 (see Recommended websites, page 73). There is also a CKD pathway, and Quality Standards 5 focuses on this disease. Patients with severe CKD lose the ability to produce erythropoietin, and so are at risk of becoming anaemic. NICE CG114 offers advice on this problem.

NICE CG73 also places importance on protein in the urine (proteinuria, detectable with dipsticks), but a better marker of renal damage is the ratio of albumin to creatinine in the urine (hence uACR). In non-diabetics, the uACR can be used to direct the use of angiotensin converting enzyme inhibitors (ACEIs) or angiotensin receptor blockers (ARBs) if the uACR is >30mg/mmol. However, in diabetics, microalbuminuria (uACR>2.5mg/mmol in men and >3.5mg/mmol in women is clinically significant. NICE CG66 on diabetes and CG34 on hypertension are also applicable.

Treatment and care of CKD is therefore conservative, and as renal function slowly deteriorates the patient should be prepared physically and psychologically for dialysis, which is generally needed when the GFR falls to about <25ml/min. The remaining treatment is transplantation.

Urate/Uric acid

This is not strictly a marker of renal function, but certainly to do with renal physiology. Uric acid and its ionised form, urate (dependent on pH), are mostly breakdown products of the synthesis of DNA, and are excreted by the kidney and in the gut. High levels can arise from increased production (maybe 10% of cases) or decreased excretion (perhaps present in 90%). Thus with poor excretion, levels in the blood will rise. Various drugs can also cause an increase in levels of this metabolite.

Urate is particularly insoluble, so when levels rise they will form crystals (e.g. in the synovial joint) and stones (e.g. in the kidney), leading to further problems such as swelling, pain and inflammation, and ultimately to an arthritis (often gout, where there can also be deposits in the skin). Risk factors for hyperuricaemia are alcoholism, use of diuretics, obesity, renal disease and heart failure.

Recommended websites

eGRF calculator using the MDRD equation:
www.renal.org/egfrcalc/

eGRF calculator using the Cockcroft-Gault equation:
www.nephron.com/cgi-bin/CGSI.cgi

NICE clinical guideline (CG) 73 on chronic kidney disease, and CG114 on the anaemia of renal disease:
www.nice.org.uk

Summary

- Although urea and creatinine are the cornerstones of the assessment of renal function, we also consider sodium and potassium.
- Increasing levels of potassium can be life-threatening.
- The gold standard test of renal function is the glomerular filtration rate, a test that requires an accurate 24-hour urine collection.
- Acute renal failure (ARF) is often associated with a greater rise in urea than the rise in creatinine.
- Chronic renal failure (CRF) is frequently characterised by a greater rise in creatinine than the rise in urea. There may also be anaemia and hypocalcaemia.
- Renal disease is frequently associated with raised uric acid, and so a gouty arthritis may develop.

Case study 5

A man, aged 75, describes making less and less urine over a period of a few days, and complains to his GP of something not right 'down there', with occasional pain. The doctor, feeling a hard mass in the lower abdomen, sends a venous sample of blood to the local District General Hospital, with the following results.

	Result (Unit)	Reference range
Na	140mmol/L	133–148
K	5.4mmol/L	3.3–5.6
Urea	56.5mmol/L	3.0–8.3
Creatinine	354μmol/L	44–133
eGFR	16ml/min/1.73m^2	<90

Clue: Compare the rise in urea to the rise in creatinine.

Interpretation

Abnormal results are raised urea and creatinine, pointing to a problem with the kidney. The increase in urea is about 10-fold over the middle of the normal range, whilst the increase in creatinine is only about 4 times. Thus the relative rise in urea is over twice the relative rise in creatinine, pointing to an initial diagnosis of an acute renal problem. This is supported by the clinical history and anuria. The eGFR is profoundly low. If chronic, this would lead to the very dangerous CKD Stage IV.

Diagnosis may be confirmed with imaging (ultrasound) and we can expect a full bladder. A most likely cause of this is blockage of the urethra, maybe by a kidney stone or stones. There seems to be no infection, and a tumour alone would be unlikely to produce such an acute picture.

8

Investigation of liver function and plasma proteins

Key words:
Bilirubin
Alkaline phosphatase (AlkPhos, or ALP)
Gamma glutamyl transpeptidase (Gamma GT)
Alanine aminotransferase (ALT)
Aspartate aminotransferase (AST)

Key pathological expressions:
Acute hepatic failure
Cholestasis
Chronic hepatic failure
Hepatitis
Jaundice

An explanation of terms:
Just as a single unit of the kidney is the nephron, a single unit of the liver is a hepatocyte (hence hepatitis [inflammation of the liver] and hepatoma [cancer of the liver], and you can guess from which organ heparin was first purified!). Like the kidney, the liver has a number of functions, but hepatic function is more diverse:

- Metabolic activity of the liver includes synthesis of a large number of different proteins, many destined for 'export' to the blood. Good examples of these are fibrinogen, C-reactive protein (CRP) and cholesterol.

- The liver converts glucose and other carbohydrates into the storage compound glycogen, and it also stores iron.

- Detoxification is another important metabolic function, ridding the body of dangerous substances such as plant and animal fungal toxins, paracetamol and alcohol. It is also where pharmaceutical drugs and anaesthetics are broken up and rendered ineffective.

Liver function tests

When red blood cells come to the end of their life, the proteins and iron in haemoglobin are recycled, but certain complex molecules (for example, bilirubin) are not. The precise biochemistry of the family of molecules is complex and beyond the scope of this text. Bilirubin, some carried by albumin, finds its way to the liver, where it is excreted via the gall bladder, bile duct and so into the intestines. However, red cells destroyed in the liver are also excreted this way. Thus, if the liver is unable to perform this function (perhaps because it is overwhelmed, or damaged), the level of bilirubin in the blood rises.

The liver synthesises and then exports a large number of proteins into the blood. If the levels of these proteins, such as albumin, fibrinogen and prothrombin, fall, we should consider failure of production. Alternatively, low levels may arise from excess consumption. However, another explanation for low levels is malnutrition, so jumping to conclusions can be dangerous!

Enzymes involved in biosynthesis and metabolism include the aminotransferases alanine aminotransferase (ALT) and aspartate aminotransferase (AST), alkaline phosphatase (AlkPhos, or ALP) and gamma-glutamyl transferase or gamma-glutamyl transpeptidase (Gamma GT, or GGT). These enzymes are the tools the liver cells use to break up large molecules into their component parts. The liver cells then use some of these parts to synthesise new molecules. Unused parts are excreted (for example, as urea and creatinine).

However, a big problem with these enzymes is that they are not only present in the liver. There are also substantial amounts of alkaline phosphatase in the bone, small intestine, placenta and kidney. Gamma GT is also widely distributed, being present in the kidney and pancreas. This enzyme is also sensitive to alcohol and certain drugs, such as phenytoin. AST and ALT are also widely distributed, being present in skeletal and cardiac muscle and in the kidney, although ALT is more liver-specific. Hence, AST may be raised following myocardial infarction.

Although it is not strictly a liver function test, now is a good time to mention alpha-feto protein (AFP), as it is raised in 80–90% of primary liver cancers (hepatoma). Levels are generally not raised when the liver carries metastatic cells from a distant primary tumour. Liver cancers, of whatever aetiology, generally display raised gamma GT, alkaline phosphatase and bilirubin.

Jaundice

This clinical sign is characterised by a yellow colouring, most evident in the sclera of the eye, and is caused by high serum bilirubin, generally greater than 40μmol/L. There is a large gap between the top end of the normal range (21μmol/L) and the most common presenting (visual) sign. However, people with a developing jaundice often have abdominal discomfort, lack of appetite, lethargy, tiredness and general non-specific illness for several days before the jaundice becomes evident. The aetiology of jaundice is most variable.

Types of liver disease

As with renal disease, we can consider pre-, true, and post-liver disease (see Figure 8, page 78).

- As mentioned earlier, when red blood cells come to the end of their lifespan they are removed from the circulation and broken up. The un-recycled part, bilirubin, remains in the blood and is eventually cleared, mostly by the liver, and some by the kidney. However, if there is excessive haemolysis, the liver is unable to keep up with purifying the blood of the high levels of bilirubin. In this case, bilirubin levels rise and can cause jaundice. Thus, there is nothing intrinsically wrong with the liver itself; it just can't keep up with the high levels of bilirubin resulting from excessive red cell destruction.

- True damage to the hepatocyte (i.e. hepatocellular damage) is often seen in, for example, cases of poisoning by inhaled solvents in paint spray, or in viral hepatitis. This would initially be characterised biochemically by increases in aminotransferases ALT and AST, and later by rising bilirubin as the excretory function of the liver is influenced.

- A good example of post-hepatic disease is obstruction or stenosis of the bile duct by factors such as gall stones, or inflammation or tumour of the head of the bile duct or pancreatic duct (cholestasis). Thus, again, the initial problem is not the tissue of the liver itself, but the associated plumbing. However, as with pre- and post-renal disease, failure to act on pre- and post-liver disease will eventually lead to true liver disease.

Aetiology of liver disease

Once again, as with renal disease, we consider the speed of onset.

Acute liver disease

Almost by definition, onset is rapid and can generally be ascribed to a single factor or event. Poisoning (e.g. organic solvents, carbon tetrachloride), drug overdose (e.g. barbiturates, herbicides), shock, severe hypoxia and acute cardiac failure are good examples of factors that precipitate acute disease. In such cases, rising levels of AST and ALT are frequently seen, followed maybe days later by bilirubin. An alternative scenario is sudden blockage of the bile duct by a stone (i.e. cholestasis). This would be more likely to be characterised by rising alkaline phosphatase and gamma GT. In some cases, viral hepatitis can be traced to a precise (infective) event.

Chronic liver disease

Again, by definition, we suspect a slow and insidious disease process, although it may also have a precise defining event, and can follow from acute disease. For example, a hepatitis virus infection may be partially treated in the short term, with a modest return of normal liver function, but chronic active hepatitis may result. A further example is cholestasis resulting from a slowly developing blockage, such as a tumour, which the surgeons may be able to treat, although (like chronic renal failure) chronic liver disease is generally irreversible.

Other common causes of chronic liver disease are alcoholism and the autoimmune disease primary biliary cirrhosis. Whatever the aetiology, the laboratory notes rising plasma markers of liver function, although in the terminal stages levels of some will fall as the liver is unable to synthesise them. Hence, there will be a risk of bleeding due to insufficient clotting proteins. Bilirubin will continue to rise and can be treated by dialysis, although this is clearly only palliative. The only effective treatment is transplantation, although this is, of course, by no means 100% successful.

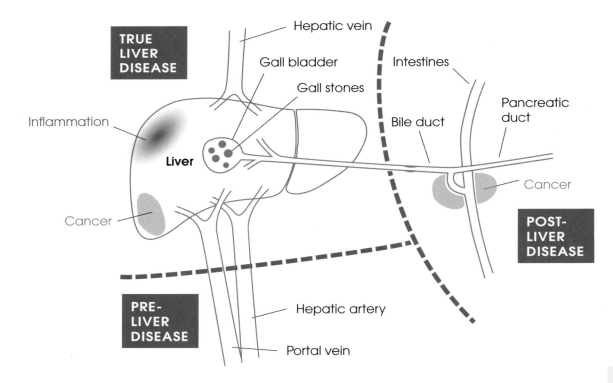

Figure 8: Aetiology of liver disease

Plasma proteins

Key words:

Total protein
Albumin
Prostate specific antigen (PSA)
C-reactive protein (CRP)
Amylase

Key pathological expressions:

Hypoalbuminaemia
Inflammation

An explanation of terms:

The laboratory offers total plasma proteins, and albumin, the latter generally making up about half of all the proteins. The remaining half is made up of dozens of other proteins (such as CRP, immunoglobulins and PSA), all at different individual concentrations. Many tumour markers are proteins.

Total proteins

As mentioned above, this global score assesses all plasma proteins. Raised total proteins can therefore (in theory) be due to any individual protein, although in practice the only protein to do this is increased levels of immunoglobulins, as may be present in an infection or in a myeloma. Decreased total protein is almost always due to hypoalbuminaemia.

Albumin

This molecule is important for a number of reasons, such as being a carrier of calcium, bilirubin and various other substances. Low levels of albumin will therefore have other consequences. Another indication of albumin's importance is in the maintenance of tissue fluid: low albumin will be a contributing factor in oedema.

Hypoalbuminaemia may be due to poor liver function, as it arises in the liver, or inadequate nutrition or malabsorption or severe nephrotic syndrome, where kidney damage is so great that albumin is lost in the urine.

C-reactive protein (CRP)

This marker of inflammation, like ESR, is typically raised in autoimmune diseases, and in bacterial infections. It will therefore often go together with a raised WBCC. Produced by the liver, by the same process that causes pyrexia, it is frequently described as an acute phase protein.

The remaining 50% or so of the total plasma protein pool is made up of numerous proteins, many of which we have already come across. These are listed in Table 8 (below). Amylase is likely to be raised in pancreatitis and pancreatic cancer.

Recommended websites

www.nhs.uk/conditions/Liver-disease/pages/introduction.aspx

www.umm.edu/ency/article/000255.htm
(Cirrhosis)

Table 8: Functions of plasma proteins

Protein	Function
Transferrin	Iron transport
Fibrinogen	Coagulation
Amylase	Pancreatic digestive enzyme
Insulin	Glucoregulatory hormone
Cancer marker	**Cancer marked**
Prostate specific antigen (PSA)	Prostate
Alpha-feto protein (AFP)	Liver
CA-125	Ovary
Immunoglobulins	Myeloma

Summary

- The aetiology of liver disease, like that of the kidney, considers pre-, true and post-hepatic causes.
- LFTs include alkaline phosphate, bilirubin, gamma GT, ALT and AST. They are used to diagnose and investigate conditions such as jaundice.
- Common causes of acute liver disease include cholestasis and viral hepatitis. Chronic liver disease often arises from alcoholism, primary biliary cirrhosis, or from acute (long-standing) hepatic damage.
- Total proteins and albumin are also important in assessing liver function. Low levels may be due to impaired synthesis and/or malnutrition.
- Many plasma proteins have identifiable functions as hormones, enzymes, or as cancer markers.

Case study 6

A male, aged 68, reports being increasingly tired and lethargic over a six-month period, with weight loss, despite his wife's attempts to 'feed him up'. More recently, he complains of abdominal discomfort. Blood results are as follows:

	Result (Unit)	Reference range
Na	138mmol/L	133–148
K	4.0mmol/L	3.3–5.6
Urea	6.1mmol/L	3.0–8.3
Creatinine	89μmol/L	44–133
eGFR	78ml/min/1.73m^2	<90
Total protein	60g/L	63–84
Albumin	28g/L	35–50
Alk phosphatase	190 IU/L	20–130
AST	89 IU/L	<37
Bilirubin	22μmol/L	<21
ALT	72 IU/L	<41
Gamma GT	215 IU/L	<64
Fibrinogen	1.3g/L	1.5–4.0
Amylase	25 IU/L	<110
CRP	2.0mg/L	<5
ESR	15mm/hour	<10

Interpretation

There are no abnormalities in the tests of renal function, so we can discount problems in this organ. However, all five liver function tests are abnormal, so this organ is clearly under suspicion. The results also show low fibrinogen and abnormal ESR but normal amylase and CRP. The abnormalities in fibrinogen, with low total protein and albumin, also indicate liver dysfunction, but the raised ESR provides little extra help. No increase in CRP points to the lack of an ongoing inflammatory response.

Additional tests would include hepatitis virus screening (A, B and C), with ultrasound imaging to check the integrity of the gall bladder. Since there is an ESR result, we must presume there is a full blood count somewhere. If not, it should certainly be ordered. The Immunology Laboratory will help with considering primary biliary cirrhosis. Additional questions to the patient may reveal use of alcohol (although, of course, this may not always be reliable). A liver biopsy may help, though this may be dangerous in view of low coagulation proteins.

9

Atherosclerosis and its risk factors

This chronic condition, characterised by damage to the blood vessel wall followed by thrombosis and hypertension, is likely to strike the majority of people in the Western world. The late stages – stroke, myocardial infarction and critical limb ischaemia (of the leg) – are almost always preceded by warning signs of transient ischaemic attack, angina and intermittent claudication. However, more pertinently, clinical disease is generally preceded by well-known risk factors: diabetes, smoking, hypertension and dyslipidaemia. The latter has replaced hypercholesterolaemia, as this incorrectly implies that all forms of cholesterol are bad (a mistaken assumption, as we shall see).

There are no direct routine laboratory tests in hypertension. Some tests can assess smoking status, although the laboratory is likely to resist such a request. The laboratory is helpful in diagnosing diabetes and hyperlipidaemia, and in the monitoring of treatment.

Diabetes mellitus

Key words:
Fasting plasma glucose
Oral glucose tolerance test (OGTT)
Glycated haemoglobin (HbA1c)

Key pathological expressions:
Diabetes mellitus
Diabetic ketoacidosis
Hyperglycaemia
Impaired fasting glycaemia
Impaired glucose tolerance

An explanation of terms:

This condition can arise without an obvious cause (i.e. primary) or may be secondary to factors such as obesity, drugs, pancreatic disease or Cushing's syndrome. It is the most common endocrine disorder, characterised by hyperglycaemia due to lack or dysfunction of insulin. Indeed, as of 2010, there were 2.6 million people in the UK known to have diabetes. Complete lack of insulin leads to insulin dependent diabetes mellitus (IDDM, about 15% of diabetics, often occurring in the young), whilst insulin resistance is the basis of non-insulin dependent diabetes mellitus (NIDDM, making up 85%, generally arising in later life and associating with obesity). As more than 50% of adults are overweight (e.g. body mass index greater than 25), there is a considerable amount of occult or pre-diabetes.

The pathology of diabetes is established: in the early stages there is hyperglycaemia with symptoms such as polyuria, polydipsia and weight loss. This leads to microvascular disease (retinopathy, neuropathy and nephropathy) and then to atherosclerosis, characterised symptomatically by coronary artery disease. Naturally, there is great variety in the presenting symptoms and rate of progression from person to person.

Blood glucose

NB: Blood glucose is perhaps the only routine biochemistry blood test that is not performed on clotted blood and needs to be taken into the anticoagulant FLOX (check with your laboratory).

Because glucose levels in the blood vary considerably during the day, the timing of the blood test is crucial, with lowest levels in the morning before eating breakfast. Hence the importance of a FASTING sample. The alternative is a random sample. Random and fasting samples are very different and therefore have different normal (target) ranges. Plasma levels also give different results from whole blood levels, so blood from the vein is different from capillary blood from a fingerprick. A fasting glucose of less than 6.1mmol/L is to be expected from non-diabetics. However, for a complete diagnosis, an oral glucose tolerance test is also performed.

The oral glucose tolerance test (OGTT)

A better method of checking a preliminary diagnosis of diabetes is with the OGTT. Using this method, the fasted subject arrives at the laboratory at perhaps 9.00 a.m., gives a blood sample, and then drinks 75g of glucose. Additional blood samples may be taken every hour up to 3 hours, and levels of glucose in the blood are plotted. However, many laboratories simply take a baseline and a 2-hour sample. A healthy response sees levels rise to a peak of less than 7.8mmol/L at 2 hours, after which time the levels fall, quite possibly back to the fasting level.

The response of a diabetic will be an increase in the glucose from a high fasting level (i.e. greater than 6.1mmol/L), which rises to peak at over 11.1mmol/L at 2 hours. Such a response is required on two separate occasions for a firm diagnosis of diabetes. However, some results do not match either of these scenarios. Figure 9 illustrates a number of alternative patterns:

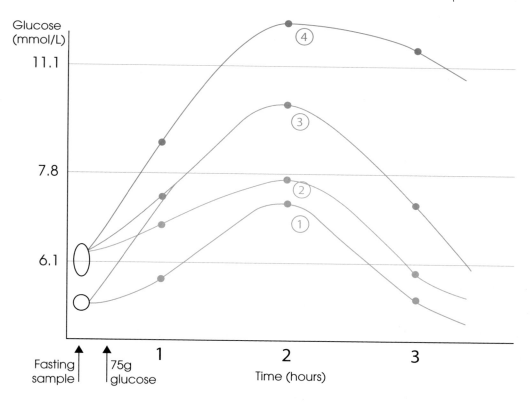

Figure 9: The oral glucose tolerance test – typical profiles

- Pattern 1 is a normal healthy response. Fasting glucose levels are low, (represented by the small circle on the left of the graph, at perhaps 4.0mmol/L). Glucose levels then rise to perhaps 7.0mmol/L at 2 hours, and then go back down to fasting levels at 3 hours.

- Pattern 2 shows impaired fasting glucose (IFG). Here, the oval on the left of the graph shows a range of high fasting levels of glucose, typically greater than 6.1mmol/L. Note that a line passes from this high fasting glucose, and peaks at around 7.6mmol/L. This is less than the threshold of 7.8mmol/L, and so it is still a normal physiological response. This proves that the individual is perfectly capable of handling the glucose challenge – their only problem is high levels when fasting.

- Pattern 3 represents impaired glucose tolerance (IGT). Some individuals, despite having a low fasting glucose (starting from the circle), have a 2-hour response that is well above the 7.8mmol/L threshold. In this example, levels are around 10mmol/L, but then fall back to the fasting levels. In other individuals, with a high fasting glucose (starting from the oval), the 2-hour peak is also above 7.8mmol/L, as in Pattern 3, so these people have both IGT and IFG.

- Pattern 4 shows the typical response of someone with diabetes mellitus. This line starts from the high fasting glucose result (the oval). It then rises rapidly to over 8mmol/L at 1 hour, and well over 11.1mmol/l at 2 hours. Levels are still high after 3 hours.

These and other data demand expert interpretation. IGT and IFG are certainly not diabetes, but they could be a risk factor for the development of classical diabetes at some time in the future. Regular monitoring and advice on weight management and diet are therefore required if diabetes is to be avoided.

Glycated haemoglobin (HbA1c)

Hyperglycaemia is not benign: it is not simply a case of having too much sugar in the blood. High sugar sticks to other proteins and cells and influences their function. One such interaction is with the haemoglobin within red blood cells. A proportion of this haemoglobin binds the glucose, and is therefore described as glycated haemoglobin (called in the laboratory HbA1c). As the glucose stays on the haemoglobin it remains there for the entire life of that red cell. Consequently, increased HbA1c indicates poor long-term control of the hyperglycaemia, and as such is useful in checking the effect of treatment over a three-month period. It follows that a high HbA1c may also be taken by many as strongly indicative of diabetes.

Diabetic ketoacidosis (DKA)

This clinical situation is found in cases of severe hyperglycaemia, and represents probably the most important crisis a diabetic can face. It is characterised by a cycle of insulin resistance and/or deficiency, with hyperglycaemia, acidosis and dehydration. Pathophysiologically, two overlapping cycles exist.

The first centres on hyperglycaemia, which invariably leads to glycosuria. It is not enough simply to excrete glucose in urine – it must be excreted with a great deal of water (thus the symptoms of polyuria), leading eventually to dehydration. The consequences of loss of blood volume include hypotension, shock and pre-renal uraemia, resulting from a fall in the glomerular filtration rate. This, in turn, leads (via several complex hormones and factors) to insulin deficiency and/or resistance, and thus back to hyperglycaemia.

Changes in the 'several complex hormones and factors' also lead to the second part of the cycle. These, alongside insulin problems, can lead to changes in lipid metabolism and the mobilisation of fatty acids from adipose tissues into the blood. Ketone bodies rise, and these can lead to acidosis with an associated hyperkalaemia. This promotes nausea and then vomiting, and so loss of fluids and eventual dehydration.

The laboratory can help in diagnosis, investigation and treatment of DKA. There are various opportunities to intervene in this cycle, with intravenous fluids to treat dehydration, and insulin to get glucose out of the blood and into cells. This hormone will also help the hyperkalaemia. If the acidosis is severe, a bicarbonate drip can be used, which may also help address the high potassium.

Hypoglycaemia

Defined by a glucose level less than 2.8 mmol/L, 99% of hypoglycaemic attacks are in patients with IDDM. Cognitive disturbances are common when levels fall below 2.0 mmol/L, followed by ECG changes, coma and death. Causes include reduced intake of carbohydrates, over-use of insulin, excess exercise or excess consumption of alcohol. Treatments include oral glucose, chocolate-rich confectionery or jam, or intramuscular injections of the hormone glucagon. However, if the patient is unconscious, intravenous glucose or dextrose will be required.

Dyslipidaemia

Key words:

Total cholesterol
HDL-cholesterol
Triglycerides
Total/HDL cholesterol ratio

Key pathological expressions:

Hypercholesterolaemia
Hypertriglyceridaemia

An explanation of terms:

The two major classes of lipids are cholesterol and triglycerides. As with diabetes, hypercholesterolaemia can be primary and secondary. The latter may be due to a poor (fat-rich) diet (with or without obesity), hypothyroidism, alcoholism, chronic renal failure or, indeed, to diabetes. The most common primary cause of raised lipids is genetic. Familial hypercholesterolaemia is the most common, but there are others, including familial hypertriglyceridaemia (raised triglycerides) and familial combined hyperlipidaemia (raised cholesterol and triglycerides).

Knowledge of serum cholesterol is necessary to be able to assess the risk of developing symptomatic atherosclerosis. Although total cholesterol is a good guide to risk, a sub-fraction, LDL-cholesterol, is more accurate. Unfortunately, LDL-cholesterol is very difficult to measure directly, but can be estimated according to a formula that consists of total cholesterol, HDL-cholesterol and triglycerides. Like glucose, levels of triglycerides can vary throughout the day so fasting levels are necessary for the most precise assessment. Should it be needed, the relevant equation for LDL is:

$$LDL = total\ cholesterol - HDL\text{-}cholesterol - (triglycerides/2.19)$$

However, this equation is only applicable to triglyceride levels that are less than 3.0 mmol/L. Of course, someone at risk of hypercholesterolaemia may well also be at risk of diabetes. For this reason, a fasting glucose sample may as well be taken at the same time.

High levels of total and LDL-cholesterol, and low HDL-cholesterol, are important as predictors of cardiovascular disease, but they are not, of course, the only such predictors – others include high blood pressure, age, male sex, smoking and diabetes. These factors can be entered into a complex formula that aims to predict and thus identify those at high risk of an adverse event (heart attack or stroke) in, shall we say, the next ten years. Other risk indicators suggest that ratio of total cholesterol to HDL should ideally be as low as possible (perhaps <2.5). Lipid-lowering therapy, such as a statin, can then be more accurately targeted.

Coronary atherosclerosis

Key words:
Creatine kinase (CK)
CK-MB
Troponin T

Key pathological expressions:
Angina
Myocardial infarction

An explanation of terms:

There are no specific laboratory tests for the presence of cerebrovascular disease (stroke), or atherosclerotic disease of the legs (as may be suggested by intermittent claudication and critical limb ischaemia). However, there are tests for the consequences of atherosclerosis of the coronary arteries, which is very likely to be present following a myocardial infarction.

These are as follows:

• Creatine kinase (CK). The heart is a heavily modified muscle, so enzymes present in damaged muscle can be expected to be raised after a heart attack. Such an enzyme is CK. However, CK is also present in skeletal muscle, so raised levels may also arise from damage to these tissues, such as may be present following heavy exercise (like running a marathon!) or in the muscle disease polymyositis. Therefore raised levels can only strictly be used with an appropriate history (including symptoms such as chest pain) and ECG changes.

• CK-MB is a variant of total CK that is much more specific for heart muscle (being absent from, for example, leg muscle), and so is more useful.

• An even more specific marker is troponin T, and another is troponin I. These are not enzymes but actual heart muscle protein, and so they are of even more precise specificity. However, Table 9 (below) provides examples of conditions where there are raised levels in the absence of a heart attack.

Table 9: Indications of raised troponins

Cardiac disease and interventions
Cardiac amyloidosis, cardiac contusion, cardiac surgery, cardioversion and implantable cardioverter defibrillator shocks, closure of atrial septal defects, coronary vasospasm, dilated cardiomyopathy, heart failure, hypertrophic cardiomyopathy, myocarditis, percutaneous coronary intervention, post-cardiac transplantation, radiofrequency ablation, supraventricular tachycardia.
Non-cardiac diseases
Critically ill patients, high dose chemotherapy, primary pulmonary hypertension, pulmonary embolism, renal failure, subarachnoid haemorrhage, scorpion envenoming, sepsis and septic shock, stroke, ultra-endurance exercise (marathon).

Source: *British Medical Journal 2004*, **328**: 1028–9.

The value of these markers has to be weighed against the time course of the reaction to the myocardial infarction: the markers' response at different times, troponins being the slowest (6–12hr) to peak. Marker use is compounded by the differences in the time that the patients present to hospital after their infarction: some will present immediately; others hours later. 'Liver' enzymes, such as alanine and aspartate aminotransferases, may also rise after an acute myocardial infarction.

Recommended websites

www.diabetes.org.uk

www.nice.org.uk/Cg71
(Clinical guideline 71 is on familial hypercholesterolaemia)

www.evidence.nhs.uk/topic/hypercholesterolaemia

www.ncbi.nlm.nih.gov/pubmedhealth/PMH0001246/

Summary

- There are no laboratory tests specific for stroke, atherosclerosis of the arteries of the legs or hypertension. The laboratory is most unlikely to agree to test for smoking.
- Diabetes can be diagnosed and monitored with fasting glucose and HbA1c. The oral glucose tolerance test is also useful, especially in clarifying the diagnosis and considering impaired glucose tolerance and impaired fasting glycaemia.
- Total cholesterol and HDL-cholesterol can be measured on a random sample; LDL-cholesterol is calculated using a formula that demands a fasting triglyceride.
- Creatine kinase (CK), CK-MB and troponins are used to help diagnose myocardial infarction.

10

Calcium, bone and musculoskeletal disease

Key words:

Calcium
Parathyroid hormone (PTH)
Albumin
Alkaline phosphatase (AlkPhos, or ALP)
Phosphate
Creatine kinase (CK)

Key pathological expressions:

Hypercalcaemia
Hypocalcaemia
Osteoporosis
Paget's disease
Rickets/Osteomalacia

An explanation of terms:

Albumin carries a great deal of calcium, so knowledge of levels of this liver protein is often required. Yes, alkaline phosphatase (ALP) features in a liver function test (LFT), but it is also present in bone, so it is also often called upon. Yes again, creatine kinase (CK) is raised after a heart attack, but it is also raised in many conditions where there is muscle damage or disease.

Calcium

This is the most abundant mineral in the body, and 99% of it is in bone. In the blood it is regulated by parathyroid hormone (PTH, arising from the parathyroid glands) acting on different tissues to raise circulating levels by increasing absorption across the gut wall, by minimising excretion, and by mobilising bone stores. Low levels of blood calcium are detected and PTH is released. As plasma calcium levels rise, this secretion is switched off – a classic example of feedback regulation.

About half of our plasma calcium circulates bound to albumin, and it is the unbound part (known as 'free' or ionised calcium) that the parathyroids respond to. This process is pH-dependent, so in acidosis the ionised calcium increases and conversely at an alkalotic pH, it falls. Consequently, in acute respiratory alkalosis, tetany may occur due to the sudden decrease in ionised calcium. The laboratory measures total calcium, i.e. free and bound, so interpretation is required. If albumin is low, total calcium may be low as a result, but the free calcium will frequently be satisfactory. Thus, such a situation is not true hypocalcaemia. If there is indeed low (total) calcium and low albumin, then a calculation is required, and the lab will do this, reporting adjusted calcium. Like almost all analytes, we consider the implications of levels above and below the reference range.

Hypercalcaemia

Present in perhaps 5% of in-patients, most cases of high plasma calcium can be explained by a small number of causes:

• Primary hyperparathyroidism results in high levels of PTH that in turn cause high blood calcium levels. This may result from a tumour of the parathyroid gland that secretes PTH.

• Malignancy: most often a tumour secreting a PTH-like protein, or else a tumour (such as a myeloma or secondaries from a breast carcinoma) that has invaded and mobilises bone to make more space for itself, resulting in calcium release from bone and its movement into the blood. In such a case there may well be low or normal PTH levels, and perhaps raised alkaline phosphatase.

• Rare reasons for high calcium include excess calcium intake, immobilisation, thyroid disease, renal disease, and inappropriate use of vitamin D, diuretics and lithium.

Since calcium is important in nerve conduction, treatment is urgently required if levels exceed 3.5mmol/L, as cardiac arrhythmias, and then arrest may follow. Treatments include vigorous rehydration, a drug from the bisphosphonate family (especially in myeloma), calcitonin and prednisolone. However, the original cause of the problem must eventually be addressed (for example, surgical excision of a PTH-secreting adenoma).

Hypocalcaemia

Remember that low calcium in itself is not necessarily true hypocalcaemia: it may be related to a low albumin, and adjusted calcium may rise to be within the normal range. Investigation centres on abnormal intake and regulation:

• Inadequate intake of calcium and/or vitamin D in the diet.

- Hypoparathyroidism results from failure of the parathyroid gland, possibly due to autoimmune disease or excessive treatment for hyperthyroidism, such as over-use of radioactive iodine or poor surgical technique.

- Renal disease: (a) this organ secretes a molecule essential for malabsorption of calcium from the intestines (i.e. secondary malabsorption); (b) damage to the nephron so that calcium is not re-absorbed from the developing urine and is thus excreted.

Like hypercalcaemia, clinical features include an abnormal ECG, and treatment must address the cause(s). Oral supplements are one avenue, synthetic vitamin D analogues another. If urgent, a calcium supplement may be added to an intravenous drip.

Phosphate

About 85% of body phosphate is in the bone, and there is a marked diurnal effect. Levels are often reciprocal with calcium. Again, we consider high and low levels:

- The most common form of hyperphosphataemia is renal failure (reduced excretion); others are hypoparathyroidism and cell lysis.

- Severe hypophosphataemia (possibly due to raised PTH) is rare, causes muscle weakness, may lead to respiratory failure, and demands urgent treatment with intravenous supplements. Other causes include treatment of diabetic ketoacidosis with insulin (as the shift of glucose into the cell may cause a similar movement of phosphates) and alkalosis.

Bone and musculoskeletal disease

Contrary to popular belief, measurement of calcium usually has little to offer the highest-profile bone disease – osteoporosis – although oral calcium supplements are advocated as a treatment. Similarly, Paget's disease is rarely characterised by abnormal calcium or phosphates but a raised alkaline phosphatase is a frequent finding, indicating increased bone turnover. However, this enzyme may also be raised in hyperparathyroidism and metastatic bone cancer.

There are no helpful blood tests to directly help the diagnosis of osteoarthritis, but lack of vitamin D causes weak, misshapen bones found in rickets (in children) and osteomalacia (in adults). As we saw in Chapter 5 (on immunology), this group includes the autoimmune conditions rheumatoid arthritis (RA), systemic lupus erythematosus (SLE), systemic sclerosis/scleroderma and ankylosing spondylitis. There are no routine blood tests for these conditions, but autoantibodies rheumatoid factor and antinuclear antibodies may be useful. However, as these diseases often have an inflammatory component, white blood cell count, ESR and CRP may be ordered.

Bear in mind that CK may also be produced by non-cardiac muscle. It may therefore be increased in conditions such as polymyositis, and can also be increased by the use of certain drugs (statins) designed to lower cholesterol.

Recommended websites

www.arthritisresearchuk.org

www.patient.co.uk/doctor/Hypercalcaemia.htm

Summary

- Almost all body calcium and phosphate is in bone; in the plasma they have a reciprocal relationship. Plasma calcium levels are regulated by feedback inhibition by PTH.
- Hypercalcaemia may be driven by inappropriately high levels of PTH or mobilisation of bone stores by a malignancy.
- Hypocalcaemia must first be checked for a low albumin and, if necessary, adjusted. Otherwise, it may be due to failure of PTH, poor diet or renal disease.
- Marked hypercalcaemia demands urgent action.
- The laboratory is unable to help in most bone conditions, except Paget's disease, where raised alkaline phosphatase alone is a frequent finding, and low levels of vitamin D in rickets/osteomalacia.
- There are no specific or routine tests for musculoskeletal disorders, but several tests can help provide a direction.

Case study 7

A 64-year-old white male presents with a developing and constant pain in his right leg. There is no erythema, swelling or cellulitis but there is muscle atrophy. The initial prescription is analgesia. A full blood count (FBC) is ordered, ESR and D-dimers are taken, and he is listed for rapid access ultrasound.

All blood results are normal, as is the ultrasound. A second round of tests is ordered – U&E's, LFTs and an X-ray of the legs. The only abnormal blood test result is raised alkaline phosphatase, and the X-ray shows slight bowing of the femur with irregular thinning of the tibia and fibula, which together make the diagnosis of Paget's disease. His treatment is a bisphosphonate drug called risedronate.

11

Investigation of thyroid function

Key words:
Free thyroxine (T4)
Thyroid stimulating hormone (TSH)

Key pathological expressions:
Thyroiditis
Thyrotoxicosis
Graves' disease
Hashimoto's disease

An explanation of terms:

The thyroid
The thyroid gland is located at the front of the neck, just below the larynx. It is a butterfly-shaped organ whose two lobes ('wings') lie to the left and right of the trachea, and are linked by an isthmus. Weighing perhaps 30g in an adult, it is composed of follicles that synthesise the two thyroid hormones, tri-iodothyronine (T3) and tetra-iodothyronine (T4, thyroxine).

The thyroid hormones have numerous influences on the metabolism of a large number of cells and tissues. Their effects include increasing basic metabolic rate, production of blood cells (especially red blood cells), regulation of fat, carbohydrate and protein synthesis and storage. They also promote cellular differentiation and growth, influence heart rate and the cardiac cycle, and even the rate of hair growth and density of sub-dermal fat.

The pituitary and hypothalamus
These tiny organs, located at the base of the brain, are constantly monitoring the levels of various blood molecules. If the need arises, they instruct other organs to make adjustments.

As far as the thyroid is concerned, the two little 'control' organs are constantly reminding this organ to make its hormones by secreting thyroid stimulating hormone (TSH).

However, if levels of T3 and T4 are low, the two control organs recognise this and increase their release of TSH. This should, in turn, cause the thyroid to increase release of its own hormones.

Conversely, if there is too much T3 and T4, this will also be noted by the pituitary and hypothalamus, and they will reduce their production of TSH. This should lead the thyroid to scale back the release of its hormones, which should then fall back to normal levels.

Iodine

This trace element is a major component of T3 and T4, and insufficient dietary iodine can cause the thyroid to swell, resulting in a goitre. However, a goitre may also be due to a tumour.

Hyperthyroidism

Present in perhaps 1% of the general population, diagnosis of this condition (also known as thyrotoxicosis) is by high T4 and low TSH. However, there are instances of normal T4 but raised T3 in some cases of hyperthyroidism. Causes of hyperthyroidism include:

- Graves' disease is the consequence of autoimmune attack on the thyroid, with the inevitable inflammation, leading to thyroiditis. It is the most common form of hyperthyroidism, accounting for perhaps 75% of cases.
- Hashimoto's thyroiditis, another type of inflammation, is caused by a different autoantibody. However, many cases of hypothyroidism are also linked to Hashimoto's disease.
- A tumour of thyroid that secretes T3 and/or T4 (that is, an adenoma).
- Sub-acute thyroiditis is characterised by a rapid presentation and often follows a viral infection, such as by the Coxsackie virus. Other forms include a postpartum thyroiditis, and a thyroiditis following mechanical damage.
- Use of certain drugs, such as amiodarone (as used in atrial fibrillation) can lead to thyroid disease. This may be because amiodarone co-incidentally structurally resembles T4. Hyperthyroidism may also be due to excessive use of thyroxine in the treatment of hypothyroidism.

Treatments include anti-thyroid dugs (e.g. carbimazole, which may also cause neutropenia, thus illustrating the close relationship between biochemistry and haematology), radioactive iodine, and surgery. Thyroid function tests are essential in monitoring these treatments.

Hypothyroidism

This is a common insidious condition with significant morbidity, and subtle and non-specific signs that are often incorrectly associated with other conditions. It is present in 35 of 10,000 people, making hypothyroidism one of the most prevalent endocrine diseases, with a frequency second only to diabetes. Indeed, it has been estimated that 3–5% of women have thyroid disease, with up to 10% of those aged over 75 years having sub-clinical hypothyroidism.

This disease is characterised by insufficient or even absent levels of TSH, T3 and/or T4. It may be due to failure of the thyroid gland itself (80–90% of cases) or the pituitary/hypothalamus (5–10%).

- The most common cause of primary hypothyroidism in the developed world is the Hashimoto's thyroiditis (as in hyperthyroidism), where the autoantibodies cause progressive destruction of thyroid tissue.

- As indicated above, hypothyroidism may be the result of over-treatment of hyperthyroidism.

- Drugs that cause hypothyroidism include lithium and amiodarone (which both reduce T3 and T4 secretion), dopamine and glucocorticoids (which decrease TSH secretion) and radioactive iodine (which destroys thyroid tissue).

Other causes include congenital hypothyroidism in infants due to the thyroid's failure to develop. Lack of treatment leads to cretinism. Diseases or injuries affecting the hypothalamus or pituitary can result in reduced production of TSH and so reduced T3 and T4.

Diagnosis also relies on T4 and TSH, but in the reverse (i.e. low T4 with high TSH). Most cases of hypothyroidism are due to destruction or failure of the thyroid gland by autoimmune mechanisms or over-treatment of hyperthyroidism. A rare cause is failure of the pituitary/hypothalamus to produce TSH. Whatever the aetiology, treatment is with thyroxine, and its effect (or lack of effect) on the thyroid is monitored with blood tests. The key features of thyroid disease are shown in Table 10 (below).

Table 10: General features of thyroid disease

	Hypothyroidism	**Hyperthyroidism**
Thyroid hormones	Low T3 and/or T4 (underactive thyroid)	High T3 and/or T4 (overactive thyroid)
Levels of TSH	Pituitary failure: low TSH Pituitary overactivity: high TSH	Pituitary failure: low TSH Pituitary excess: high TSH
Common signs and symptoms	Lethargy, dry coarse and pale skin, slow speech and mental function, pallor, hoarse voice, lethargy, constipation	Increased irritability and sweating, tremor, lethargy, breathlessness, muscle weakness
The heart, temperature control, and weight	Bradycardia, cold intolerance and cool extremities, weight gain	Tachycardia, palpitations, arrhythmia, heat intolerance and warm extremities, weight loss
Treatment	Replacement therapy (oral thyroxine)	Suppression of the thyroid (drugs, surgery, radioactive iodine)
Allied clinical conditions	Myxodema, goitre, Hashimoto's thyroiditis, anaemia	Exopthalmia, goitre, Hashimoto's thyroiditis, Graves' disease

Recommended websites

www.british-thyroid-association.org

www.bft-thyroid.org

Summary

- The laboratory generally offers free T4 and TSH.
- Hyperthyroidism is most often characterised by high T4 and low TSH.
- Hypothyroidism is generally associated with low T4 but high TSH.

Case study 8

A 34-year-old man complains of weight loss, palpitations at night, sweats, anxiety and a dry mouth. His girlfriend adds that he talks much more rapidly than he did six months ago. On examination, he is indeed sweaty but his body temperature is not raised. However, blood pressures are 143/86 and the pulse rate is 93 beats per minute. You order thyroid function tests.

	Result (unit)	Reference range
TSH	<0.1mU/L	0.27–4.2
T3	9.5pmol/L	4.0–6.5
T4	31.2pmol/L	12–22

The case is clearly hyperthyroid. You order an antibody screen, which reveals antibodies to the surface of thyroid cells, consistent with a diagnosis of Graves' disease. You start him on 30 mg carbimazole daily, which produces no ill effects after four weeks' treatment. The patient feels better after only three weeks, and after six weeks his blood profile, blood pressure and tachycardia have all improved. After six months, a trial of a reduced dose is recommended, as long-term high dose carbimazole use may burn out the thyroid and render the patient hypothyroid. Most patients are maintained on a dose of 5–15mg daily.

12

Blood gases and pH

Key words:

Hydrogen ions (H$^+$)
pH
Bicarbonate (HCO$_3^-$)
Blood carbon dioxide (PCO$_2$) Blood oxygen (PO$_2$)

Key pathological expressions:

Metabolic acidosis
Metabolic alkalosis
Respiratory acidosis
Respiratory alkalosis

An explanation of terms:

The P in PO$_2$ and PCO$_2$ indicates partial pressure. Rarely, total CO$_2$ may be requested, being the sum of dissolved CO$_2$, carbonic acid and bicarbonate. However, 95% of this total value is contributed by the bicarbonate. PO$_2$ is often used to monitor the efficiency of oxygen therapy. In blood gas analysis, the bicarbonate is not measured directly but is calculated from the H$^+$ and the PCO$_2$ alone, in contrast to 'normal' serum biochemistry, where bicarbonate is measured directly.

As discussed earlier, the waste products of our normal metabolism include urea and creatinine, to which we can now add hydrogen ions (H$^+$) and carbon dioxide (CO$_2$). The former is excreted in urine, the latter at the lungs in our exhaled breath. It follows that disease in either organ will lead to changes in these blood components. Levels of H$^+$ being too high, and thus the pH being low (tending to, or lower than, pH 7), is acidosis. Conversely, when the pH is high (tending to, or exceeding pH 7.6), with low levels of H$^+$, there is likely to be alkalosis. However, the picture is complex and therefore requires some explanation.

Hydrogen ions can exist by themselves or as part of water, and increased H^+ leads to a low pH and acidosis. However, CO_2 is part of the system, as it can combine with water to give carbonic acid, in the following equation:

$$H_2O + CO_2 \rightleftharpoons H_2CO_3$$

This indeed is how a great deal of carbon dioxide is carried from the tissues to the lungs in red blood cells. The carbonic acid, acting as a weak acid, can itself break down to a hydrogen ion and the bicarbonate ion:

$$H_2CO_3 \rightleftharpoons H^+ + HCO_3^-$$

The regulation (homeostasis) of this system is quite robust, and various checks and balances are in place (mostly in the kidney) to ensure that the status quo is maintained. For example, there are various buffer systems (such as bicarbonate, phosphate, haemoglobin and proteins) designed to keep the level of H^+ acceptable. For example, if the level of H^+ falls, more can be generated from carbonic acid. When carbonic acid itself runs low, more can be generated from water and carbon dioxide.

When this system breaks down, the result is acidosis or alkalosis. The primary pathology can depend on respiratory disorders, where the primary pulmonary defect in ventilation affects the PCO_2. An alternative is a metabolic disorder, of which there may be several, such as production of, or ingestion of, certain acids (in such doses that the kidney and/or buffering systems cannot cope), the loss of H^+, and the loss or retention of bicarbonate. Thus, two types of both acidosis and alkalosis are recognised.

Acidosis (raised plasma H^+)

Metabolic acidosis is characterised by an increased production and/or decreased excretion of H^+. Due to complex buffering with bicarbonate, levels of the latter may fall, and there may well be a compensatory hyperventilation that will lead to a fall in CO_2. Examples of clinical syndromes increasing H^+ include diabetic and alcoholic ketoacidosis, lactic acidosis and poisoning by methanol, salicylate or ingestion of acids. Renal failure will lead to failure to excrete H^+, whilst bicarbonate can be lost in severe diarrhoea.

Respiratory acidosis (raised PCO_2) is caused by an increase (probably due to retention) of CO_2. This in turn may be due to hypoventilation, itself possibly caused by drugs (e.g. narcotics, anaesthetics), nerve damage (motor neurone disease, poliomyelitis) or muscle problems, stroke and trauma. Respiratory diseases causing acidosis include bronchitis, asthma, fibrosis, and chronic obstructive airways disease (COAD).

Alkalosis (decreased plasma H$^+$)

Metabolic alkalosis (with raised bicarbonate) is often due to loss of H$^+$ from the gastro-intestinal tract by vomiting and diarrhoea. Certain drugs (e.g. thiazide diuretics) may cause H$^+$ to be lost in urine. Because ventilation is generally normal, PCO_2 levels can be unchanged (or modestly raised) and so bicarbonate rises. Another cause is excess ingestion of alkali solutions (e.g. sodium bicarbonate solution by athletes).

Respiratory alkalosis is due to hyperventilation, so PCO_2 falls. The bicarbonate is generally normal. This may be voluntary, mechanical, or due to stimulation of the brain stem respiratory centre (by pain, drugs, fever, hypoxia due to high altitude, anaemia and/or pulmonary disease and oedema giving poor perfusion).

Blood sampling

Generally speaking, the greatest call for blood gases is in Accident and Emergency, Intensive Care, Neonatal Units, and in Surgery, and is often required urgently. Because of the large gradient in oxygen and carbon dioxide between venous and arterial blood, the latter is used. However, the gases in blood can exchange with those in the air. The test must therefore be done rapidly, and so the blood gas analysers are generally sited close to where they are needed (although the Pathology Laboratory may also have an analyser). If blood is to be sent to the laboratory, it should be carried rapidly in a capped, heparinised syringe, and ideally in crushed ice.

Clinical interpretation

First, consider the H$^+$ level, which defines acidosis or alkalosis. Next, look at the PCO_2, and then, if necessary, the level of bicarbonate and PO_2. Interpretation can then follow.

1. **Increased H$^+$: therefore acidosis**

    1.1 Decreased PCO_2, therefore metabolic acidosis. Bicarbonate is also generally reduced.

1.2 Normal PCO_2, therefore uncompensated metabolic acidosis. This is likely to be because this is a simultaneous respiratory acidosis with retention of CO_2. Plasma bicarbonate will be reduced.

1.3 Increased PCO_2, therefore respiratory acidosis. If this is simple, bicarbonate will be high. However, if acute, there can be raised H^+, PCO_2 and bicarbonate (slightly) as the renal responses have yet to develop.

2. Normal H^+

This does not always mean there are no metabolic problems: there may be two concurrent competing problems. For example:

2.1 Decreased PCO_2, possibly because of a mixed respiratory alkalosis and metabolic acidosis. Bicarbonate is generally reduced.

2.2 Normal PCO_2, therefore no acid/base disturbance.

2.3 Increased PCO_2, therefore either a fully compensated respiratory acidosis, or a mixed respiratory acidosis and a concurrent metabolic alkalosis. Both lead to a raised level of bicarbonate.

3. Decreased H^+: therefore alkalosis

3.1 Decreased PCO_2, therefore respiratory alkalosis. If this is uncomplicated, bicarbonate will also be decreased.

3.2 Normal PCO_2, therefore uncompensated metabolic alkalosis. Plasma bicarbonate will be increased.

3.3 Increased PCO_2, therefore another complex disturbance such as metabolic alkalosis with some respiration changes (i.e. hypoventilation) in compensation. Plasma bicarbonate will also be increased.

Management

First, understand the aetiology and define the underlying cause. If this is not immediately possible, neutralisation of the pH problem should be undertaken. A short-term treatment of acute and profound acidosis of either form is intravenous bicarbonate to mop up the excess H^+ ions and restore the pH. However, sooner or later the cause must be addressed. In respiratory acidosis, the objective is to improve alveolar ventilation and so lower the PCO_2, possibly by mechanical means, or by giving oxygen. A saline drip (possibly with potassium supplementation) may be useful to stimulate renal perfusion. A common treatment for the hyperventilation of respiratory alkalosis is to get the subject to breathe into a paper bag. This will generally force more CO_2 in inspired air, and thus into the blood.

Recommended websites

www.patient.co.uk/doctor/Metabolic-Acidosis.htm

www.rightdiagnosis.com/a/alkalosis/symptoms.htm

www.labtestsonline.org.uk/understanding/conditions/acidosis/

Summary

- Arterial blood must be measured as soon as possible after it has been obtained, and must be transported in ice.
- Acidosis can be respiratory (e.g. following lung disease as in COAD [chronic obstructive airways disease]) or metabolic (due to over-production of, and/or failure to excrete H^+).
- Alkalosis can be respiratory (e.g. due to hyperventilation) or metabolic (e.g. loss of gastric secretions).
- A simple treatment of acidosis is with an infusion of bicarbonate. Treatment of respiratory alkalosis is by breathing into a paper bag, and of metabolic alkalosis by addressing the root cause.

Part 3

Case reports

13

Case reports in primary care

There is a growing trend for patients to be investigated and managed within their own General Practice. Any appropriately trained practitioner can take and order blood tests, which may then be sent to the local Pathology Laboratory for analysis. The lab returns the results, often by email. It is then for the practitioner to interpret and act on these results. The following scenarios reflect this process.

To aid clarity, units for the results are not shown. If needed, they are listed on pages 142–4. However, remember that reference ranges differ between individual laboratories, so those provided in this book cannot be used in your own practice.

Case report 1

A 69-year-old man pops into a Well Man Clinic whilst out shopping with his wife. He generally considers himself to be in good health, being a non-smoker, physically active (playing golf twice a week) and not overweight. His blood results are passed to the General Practice for your interpretation.

Test	Reference range	Result	Test	Reference range	Result
Na	133–148	138	K	3.3–5.6	3.8
Urea	3.0–8.3	5.3	Creatinine	44–133	92
T protein	63–84	69	Albumin	35–50	39
Calcium	2.2–2.6	2.75	Gamma GT	<64	55
Bilirubin	<21	9	Alk phos	20–130	145
ALT	<41	30	PSA	<4.0	2
Cholesterol	2.5–5.0	6.7	Triglycerides	<2.3	2.85
Glucose	<6.1	7.0	CRP	<5	1.5

Haemoglobin	133–167	146	Red cell count	4.3–5.7	5.1
MCV	80–98	86.5	White cell count	4–10	6.5
Neutrophils	1.7–6.1	4.5	Lymphocytes	1.0–3.2	1.5
ESR	<10	12	Platelets	150–400	265

Interpretation

Abnormal results are calcium, alkaline phosphatase, cholesterol, triglycerides and glucose. Normal LFTs and normal renal function (eGFR 75ml/min/1.73m² = Stage II CKD) exclude these organs as the source of raised alkaline phosphatase. Triglycerides and glucose could be raised because this is almost certainly a non-fasting sample. A repeat (fasting) test, to include PTH, is needed to confirm the abnormalities and help explain the raised calcium. HDL-cholesterol also needs to be determined. A 'bone' problem may be present. The high cholesterol probably needs to be treated, initially by a three-month trial of a low-fat diet. Without blood pressure or smoking history, we cannot say if this individual is at a high risk of a cardiovascular event, but if the high cholesterol is genuine, statins are likely to be offered.

Case report 2

A female, aged 53 years, is married with three children. A frequent blood donor, she reported several months of general tiredness and malaise when attending for a donor session. Found to be slightly anaemic, her donation was politely rejected and she was advised to visit her GP. The following results are returned for your interpretation.

Test	Reference range	Result	Test	Reference range	Result
Na	133–148	136	K	3.3–5.6	4.8
Urea	3.0–8.3	6.3	Creatinine	44–133	104
T protein	63–84	65	Albumin	35–50	42
Calcium	2.2–2.6	2.82	PTH	7–53	65
Bilirubin	<21	12	Alk phos	20–130	105
ALT	<41	25	Gamma GT	<45	30
Free T4	12–22	3	TSH	0.3–4.2	7.5

Haemoglobin	118–148	106	Red cell count	3.9–5.0	4.0
MCV	80–98	91.0	White cell count	4–10	5.4
Neutrophils	1.7–6.1	3.5	Lymphocytes	1.0–3.2	1.6
ESR	<10	16	Platelets	150–400	225

Interpretation

Consider first that her symptoms may reflect the menopause, but this will not influence the laboratory results. Sodium, potassium, urea and creatinine are all acceptable, suggesting good renal function, although the eGFR is 51ml/min/1.73m^2 (Stage III CKD). Both calcium and PTH are raised, and the low T4 with high TSH suggests hypothyroidism. Liver function tests and proteins are normal. The high calcium is certainly a concern and demands investigation. Given the physical location of the parathyroids, the thyroid problem (possibly autoimmune in origin) may be causing the calcium irregularities.

Blood donors are screened for low haemoglobin, confirmed with the formal test, and the abnormal ESR confirms a pathology. This may be linked to the hypothyroidism, as T4 can act as a growth factor to stimulate red cell production. Referral to an endocrinologist is required, and the endocrinologist will establish the extent of the thyroid and parathyroid pathology.

Case report 3

A male, aged 37 years, a frequent traveller abroad, visits his family doctor with a long history of feeling generally tired and unwell, but without any precise symptoms. On examination, there is tenderness on the right side of the abdomen. His diet is good, he reports no sweating or fevers, and there are no changes in his bowel habits or frequency of urination.

Test	Reference range	Result	Test	Reference range	Result
Na	133–148	136	K	3.3–5.6	4.9
Urea	3.0–8.3	6.2	Creatinine	44–133	88
T protein	63–84	75	Albumin	35–50	40
Bilirubin	<21	25	Alk phos	20–130	155
ALT	<41	45	Gamma GT	<64	154
CRP	<5	6.5	AST	<35	43

Haemoglobin	133–167	152	Red cell count	4.3–5.7	5.5
MCV	80–98	88.0	White cell count	4–10	8.9
Neutrophils	1.7–6.1	5.8	Lymphocytes	1.0–3.2	1.9
Monocytes	0.2–0.6	0.6	Eosinophils	0.03–0.46	0.6
ESR	<10	15	Platelets	150–400	312

Interpretation

The renal profile is good but there is evidence of liver problems with all tests being abnormal. The history suggests a long-term problem and questioning would have considered anything that would have provoked an acute insult. Other, more intrusive questioning may be required, and supportive tests such as ultrasound would help. Differential diagnoses include poor outflow of bile from the gall bladder (perhaps due to an obstruction) or maybe a tumour at the head of the bile duct, or maybe alcoholism. A hepatitis virus screen should certainly be done, as this may indicate a low-grade infection, or perhaps even chronic active hepatitis. Is the frequent foreign travel relevant?

The haematology profile is normal except for a monocytosis, an eosinophilia and a raised ESR. The white cell abnormalities could at a push be coincidental, but alongside the ESR are likely to be pathological. Is there a parasite present? Yes, the total white cell count is within range, but the neutrophil count is close to the top of the reference values. All tests should be repeated and, in addition, the patient should be tested for hepatitis virus infection.

Case report 4

Part 1

A female, aged 59 years, reported progressive weight loss and tiredness over six to nine months. Over the last three months she also noted a growing mass in the right iliac fossa, but no pain, and even more recently was becoming 'unwell'. On examination, there was also a mild splenomegaly.

Test	Reference range	Result	Test	Reference range	Result
Na	133–148	147	K	3.3–5.6	5.2
Urea	3.0–8.3	7.9	Creatinine	44–133	129
T protein	63–84	66	Albumin	35–50	33
Calcium	2.2–2.6	2.65			

Bilirubin	<21	10	Alk phos	20–130	706
ALT	<41	30	CA-125	0–30	580
Cholesterol	2.5–5.0	4.5	Triglycerides	<2.3	2.71
TSH	0.3–4.2	7.3	Free T4	12–22	4
Haemoglobin	118–148	110	Red cell count	3.9–5.0	3.7
MCV	80–98	88.8	White cell count	4–10	7.8
Neutrophils	1.7–6.1	5.0	Lymphocytes	1.0–3.2	2.0
ESR	<10	15	Platelets	150–400	213

Interpretation

All renal indices are within the reference range, though at the high end of the scale, giving eGFR 39ml/min/1.73m^2 = Stage III CKD. Albumin is a little low, with marginally raised calcium. The most abnormal routine result is the markedly raised alkaline phosphatase, but this pales into insignificance compared to the very high CA-125, a marker (principally) of ovarian cancer, but also present in cervical, breast, bowel and other cancers. Thyroid tests are consistent with hypothyroidism, and the haematology results support the diagnosis of normocytic anaemia, possibly secondary to the hypothyroidism and/or the presumed cancer.

There is a clear urgent need for referral to the local oncology service to determine the cause of the raised CA-125. The other abnormalities (such as the thyroid question) will be addressed in turn. The isolated raised alkaline phosphatase does not reflect liver disease and may be related to the cancer.

Part 2

The same woman returns 18 months later, with vague and non-specific symptoms, complaining of feeling unwell.

Test	Reference range	Result	Test	Reference range	Result
Na	133–148	139	K	3.3–5.6	4.1
Urea	3.0–8.3	3.5	Creatinine	44–133	93
T protein	63–84	63	Albumin	35–50	33
Calcium	2.2–2.6	2.45			

Bilirubin	<21	15	Alk phos	20–130	90
ALT	<41	35	Gamma GT	<45	164
AST	<37	23	Cholesterol	2.5–5.0	4.0
Triglycerides	<2.3	2.88			

Haemoglobin	118–148	120	Red cell count	3.9–5.0	4.3
MCV	80–98	97.1	White cell count	4–10	5.2
Neutrophils	1.7–6.1	3.2	Lymphocytes	1.0–3.2	1.4
ESR	<10	12	Platelets	150–400	274

Interpretation

We presume the woman has had treatment for unspecified abdominal cancer (bowel/ovary). The abnormalities are (as initially) a low albumin and raised triglycerides, but there is a new raised gamma GT. In comparison with the initial result, renal function has improved (eGFR 57 ml/min/1.73m^2) and the low red cell indices, hypercalcaemia and raised alkaline phosphatase have all resolved. It is tempting to speculate that this is the result of the (surgical?) treatment of the cancer.

However, the raised gamma GT is annoying, and may perhaps be a late effect of chemotherapy or radiotherapy to the liver, though this seems unlikely as this is only the abnormal LFT. The same argument applies to the hypothesis of liver metastases. We need another CA-125 result. However, an alternative explanation is simple excess alcohol intake: this in itself causes gamma GT and triglycerides to rise. Alcohol also increases the MCV, as seems likely in this case. Looking again, we see the cholesterol has fallen by 0.5mmol/L, and the bilirubin has increased by 50%, which may support the alcohol hypothesis, although this may reflect a degree of malnutrition. Use of alcohol is a common psychological prop after cancer surgery, and a referral to counselling may be a good move.

Case report 5

Interpret these oral glucose tolerance tests. Data are the serial levels of glucose (units: mmol/L) after the 75g of glucose taken orally.

Case and notes	Pre-load glucose	1 hour later	2 hours later	3 hours later
1. Male, 65, obese, often tired and thirsty, with some diarrhoea	8.1	11.5	16.2	12.2
2. Male, 41, dipstick glycosuria found at a Well Man Clinic	6.5	7.8	8.9	7.4
3. Female, 62, complains of a dry mouth and skin, and hair loss	7.4	12.8	14.7	9.9
4. Male, 25, high fingerprick glucose at a church fête	4.2	6.2	6.9	5.2
5. Female, 75, high random glucose on GP's clinic machine	6.3	7.0	7.6	6.9

Interpretation

Cases 1 and 3 are both barn-door diabetes, with high fasting and high 2-hour levels of glucose. The second case is impaired glucose tolerance, with the 2-hour result between 7.7 and 11.1mmol/L. Case 4 shows no signs of a glucose problem with a normal response, suggesting the church fête result was incorrect. Case 5 has a good 2-hour response (<7.8mmol/L) but a high fasting result, hence impaired fasting glycaemia. NB: An alternative definition of diabetes is a high HbA1c, perhaps >48mmol/mol/6.5%, but you need to refer to local guidelines.

Case report 6

An 82-year-old man presents with a four-month history of excessive and progressive tiredness and lethargy, and occasional pain in some bones, but not his joints. During the recent winter, he twice needed antibiotics to treat a chest infection. On examination, he was thin, pale and with a small lump in his left axilla. The blood test results were as follows:

Test	Reference range	Result	Test	Reference range	Result
Haemoglobin	133–167	98	White cell count	4.0–10.0	8.0
RCC	4.3–5.7	4.1	MCV	77–98	82.5
Platelets	140–400	157	ESR	<10	85

Neutrophils	2.0–7.0	3.2	Lymphocytes	1.0–3.0	3.8
Monocytes	0.2–1.0	0.3	Eosinophils	0.02–0.5	0.15
Basophils	0.02–0.1	0.05	Atypical cells	<0.02	0.5
Na	133–144	139	K	3.4–5.1	4.8
Urea	3.0–8.3	7.5	Creatinine	44–133	121
Total protein	60–80	85	Calcium	2.2–2.6	2.75
Albumin	35–50	38			
Bilirubin	<21	12	Alk phos	20–130	145
AST	10–50	20	ALT	5–42	32
Gamma GT	<70	54	CRP	<5.0	7.2

Interpretation

There are many abnormalities. These are low haemoglobin and red cells, with high ESR, lymphocytes, atypical leukocytes (which exceed the number of monocytes), total protein, calcium, alkaline phosphatase and CRP. eGFR is 53ml/min/1.73m^2, giving Stage III CKD.

With low red cell indices and a history of tiredness and lethargy, the patient is anaemic, and an MCV in the reference range makes this a normocytic anaemia. The greatest abnormality is the ESR, one of the primary reasons for which is rheumatoid arthritis. However, with no history of overt joint pains, we can probably exclude this. Although the lymphocyte count is raised, this could conceivably be due to an infection, but few infections can, by themselves, cause such a grossly abnormal ESR. The increased number of atypical leukocytes demands attention.

The key abnormalities are the raised alkaline phosphatase, calcium and total protein. These results would prompt a second round of investigations: the raised calcium may be due to mobilisation from bone or may be due to primary hyperparathyroidism, which would be helped by knowledge of the PTH concentration. An alternative is that the hypercalcaemia is due to bone metastases, a possible source being the prostate, hence the request for the measurement of PSA. The hyperproteinaemia would prompt a request for serum protein electrophoresis.

A low PTH rules out primary hyperparathyroidism as a cause of the hypercalcaemia, and a low PSA would also effectively rule out prostate cancer. But a key test is electrophoresis, which, if reporting a paraprotein, effectively makes the diagnosis of myeloma. This would account for the abnormal ESR with high calcium and alkaline phosphatase. The normocytic anaemia is an established aspect of this, whilst the raised lymphocyte count and atypical cells may be due to some plasma cells that have escaped the bone marrow.

Other useful investigations would be X-rays and bone scans to assess how far the tumour has infiltrated the skeleton. However, treatment is likely to be palliative.

Case report 7

A 63-year-old man with type 2 diabetes, a body mass index of 28.5kg/m^2, mildly reduced renal function, and a below–the-knee amputation, is seen at his home by the community matron. She is concerned that his remaining foot feels cool and looks pale, and she takes some blood. Whilst she is doing so, the patient recalls that a blood test was done 'months and months ago'. On examination today, his systolic/diastolic blood pressure is 142/82mmHg. His medications are amlodipine 5mg once a day, frusemide 40mg twice a day, ramipril 5mg once a day, simvastatin 20mg once a day and metformin 1000mg once a day. A week later the District Nurse telephones and asks for an opinion. You review his blood results and compare them with bloods taken nine months earlier.

Test	Reference range	9 months ago	Now
Haemoglobin	133–167	132	129
MCV	80–98	85.5	86.4
Red cell count	4.3–5.7	4.9	4.7
Haematocrit	0.35–0.55	0.42	0.41
Platelets	140–400	296	301
ESR	<10	8	12
HbA1c	20–40	71	78
White cell count	3.7–9.5	7.6	7.9
Neutrophils	1.7–6.1	5.0	5.6
Lymphocytes	1.0–3.2	2.0	1.8

Sodium	133–144	138	141
Potassium	3.4–5.1	4.4	5.0
Urea	3.0–8.3	9.1	9.3
Creatinine	44–133	112	168
Bilirubin	<21	9	12
Gamma GT	<70	35	45
AST	<60	43	38
Alk phosphatase	20–130	120	112
Total protein	63–84	68	65
Albumin	35–50	33	29
uACR	<2.5	3.6	8.3
Total cholesterol	2.5–5.0	4.9	5.1
HDL-cholesterol	>1.2	1.4	1.3

Interpretation

The low haemoglobin and normal MCV point to a normocytic anaemia at both time points. The HbA1c is high in the initial sample and has increased further in the second sample, indicating deteriorating glycaemic control. Nine months ago, the marginally acceptable total cholesterol has gone out of range. Regarding renal function, the urea is consistently high, but the creatinine has deteriorated markedly: the eGFR (ideally >90ml/min/1.73m^2) has fallen from 61 to 38. The albumin has fallen and the uACR has become considerably worse.

The health of this diabetic seems have deteriorated markedly in the nine months between the samples. Haemoglobin is definitely low and the patient is likely to be anaemic, and the HbA1c has become more adverse. Anaemia is not uncommon in diabetes, but a clear link is often uncertain. However, the most concerning aspect is the rise in creatinine and parallel fall in eGFR. This gives a clear diagnosis of chronic renal failure, and this has progressed from Stage II, straight through Stage IIIa, to Stage IIIb, and is mirrored by the adverse uACR. The latter may be linked to the reduction in serum albumin, which may be because of loss into the urine through a damaged glomerulus.

Risk factor management

There are several aspects needing attention. This patient needs a lower total cholesterol, certainly <4.5mmol/L, maybe even <4mmol/L, which should be achieved by increasing the simvastatin to 40mg a day. Similarly, the blood pressure target in general health of <140/90 is lower in high-risk groups, and should be <135/85, although as an amputee and therefore with a history of atherosclerosis perhaps a target of <130/80. There may also be a need to juggle those drugs (such as ACE inhibitor ramipril) whose plasma levels are influenced by renal function. This patient is at risk of suffering a major cardiovascular event (myocardial infarction, stroke) and would certainly benefit from 75mg aspirin daily. Finally, the hyperglycaemia needs to be addressed, and there are a number of options, including insulin, which is normally reserved for type 1 diabetics. There may also be a case for a visit to a Day Hospital, where consultants can meet in a multi-disciplinary team to discuss options.

NICE guidelines CG127 (on hypertension), CG87 (newer agents in diabetes), CG119 (diabetic foot problems) and CG67 (lipid modification) apply.

Case report 8

A 48-year-old woman with a body mass index of 26.5kg/m^2 complains of generalised aches and pains (which are getting worse), with some early morning stiffness, especially in her legs and the back. On examination, there is some eczema. She is advised to take simple analgesics, take regular exercise and lose weight. A blood test is taken for rheumatoid factor, which comes back as negative.

Six months later she returns, saying the pains have got worse, and are now in both left and right wrists, and some finger joints in both hands. She is also on the maximum dose of paracetamol. On examination, there is also tenderness in various muscles. The rheumatoid factor is repeated, and comes back weakly positive. All this prompts a full haematology, biochemistry and immunology screen aimed at a connective tissue disease.

Test	Reference range	Result	Test	Reference range	Result
Haemoglobin	118–148	121	Red cell count	3.9–5.0	4.2
MCV	77–98	84.6	ESR	<10	21
White cell count	4.0–10.0	7.9	Neutrophils	2.0–7.0	5.5
Lymphocytes	1.0–3.0	1.9	Platelets	143–400	367

Na	133–144	140	K	3.4–5.1	4.4
Urea	3.0– 8.3	6.7	Creatinine	44–133	89
Bilirubin	< 21	10	ALP	20–130	45
AST	10–50	21	ALT	5–42	27
Gamma GT	<70	45	HsCRP	<3.5	v
Rheumatoid factor	<20 IU/mL	45 IU/mL	Antinuclear antibodies	negative	negative

Interpretation

The initial presenting symptoms are vague, but with hindsight they were clear harbingers of something more sinister, and it is likely that this woman is suffering from an inflammatory connective tissue disease. The only very slightly raised body mass index is likely to exclude osteoarthritis (overweight/obesity being the greatest risk factor). This exclusion is supported by the raised ESR, as osteoarthritis is a disease whose inflammation is limited to the joint and has minimal systemic effects.

The most common disease in this group is rheumatoid arthritis, commonly attacking middle-aged women, and the positive rheumatoid factor and history point to this diagnosis. Note the qualification of 'point to', as the sensitivity and specificity of several autoantibodies tests (including rheumatoid factor) are far from 100%. Indeed, in this report, only a result of >40 IU/mL is significant, and our patient's result only slightly exceeds this. Consequently the ultimate diagnosis demands both clinical and laboratory features, according to guidelines such as those of the American College of Rheumatology and the European League Against Arthritis (EULAR). The raised CRP indicates ongoing inflammation, as part of an acute phase response. The red cell indices are within reference values, but are low, and may fall, leading to the anaemia of chronic diseases.

Management will focus on reducing the laboratory markers, which are assumed to be surrogates of disease severity. NICE clinical guideline CG79 (rheumatoid arthritis) applies.

14

Case reports in secondary care

Almost by definition, these cases are likely to be more serious, and so the diagnosis must be determined rapidly and accurately. The on-site Pathology Laboratory and other resources provide crucial help. As for the primary care reports, units for these results are (generally) not shown. If needed, they are presented on page 142. Again, remember that reference ranges differ between laboratories, and so the ones listed in this book cannot be used in your own practice.

Case report 9

A man of unknown age, but looking perhaps 50, was brought to Accident and Emergency by the police, having been found collapsed. He was poorly dressed, unshaven and unkempt. On examination, there was no evidence of violence, concussion or alcohol abuse, but he was thin and incommunicative with dry lips and tongue. His pulse was 104, and his blood pressure was 95/65.

Test	Reference range	Result	Test	Reference range	Result
Na	133–148	155	K	3.3–5.6	4.6
Urea	3.0–8.3	22.9	Creatinine	44–133	155
T protein	63–84	58	Albumin	35–50	31
Bilirubin	<21	9	Alk phos	20–130	145
ALT	<41	26	Gamma GT	<64	45
Glucose	<6.1	2.8	CRP	<5	1.5
Haemoglobin	133–167	136	Red cell count	4.3–5.7	6.0
MCV	80–98	93.5	White cell count	4–10	5.8
Neutrophils	1.7–6.1	3.9	Lymphocytes	1.0–3.2	1.4
ESR	<10	5	Platelets	150–400	225

Interpretation

This is a reasonably clear case of dehydration, where the clinical signs and laboratory tests concur. There is pre-renal uraemia (and so acute renal failure), low total protein and low albumin. LFTs are acceptable and the normal glucose excludes coma linked to diabetic ketoacidosis. Renal function is poor, with eGFR 44ml/min/1.73m^2 = Stage III CKD. The red cell count is a little raised (erythrocytosis) and this may also reflect the dehydration. It therefore looks like self-neglect, possibly with malnutrition. After bed rest with rehydration, a referral to Social Services seems appropriate.

Case report 10

A 55-year-old male cave explorer was trapped for seven hours after the roof of a cave collapsed on him. When rescued, he was in marked pain and was immediately given analgesia, as he was suspected of having sustained fractures and crush injuries to his back and legs. In A&E, he was disorientated and confused with rapid breathing, a pulse of 110 and systolic/diastolic blood pressures of 100/70mmHg. Blood gases were normal and he was adequately oxygenated (pulse oximetry 98%). Bloods were taken, a saline drip put up, and he was sent to X-ray. As he returned, the following bloods were available on the hospital pathology webpage.

Test	Reference range	Result	Test	Reference range	Result
Na	133–148	151	K	3.3–5.6	6.3
Urea	3.0–8.3	7.9	Creatinine	44–133	123
T protein	63–84	72	Albumin	35–50	42
Bilirubin	<21	19	Alk phos	20–130	125
ALT	<41	35	Gamma GT	<64	54
Cholesterol	2.5–5.0	6.7	Triglycerides	<2.3	2.85
Glucose	<6.1	2.9	Creatine kinase	<150	225
CK-MB	<25	13			

Haemoglobin	133–167	150	Red cell count	4.3–5.7	5.5
MCV	80–98	91.6	White cell count	4–10	8.5
Neutrophils	1.7–6.1	6.5	Lymphocytes	1.0–3.2	2.0
ESR	<10	8	Platelets	150–400	325

Interpretation

With such a history, we can expect multiple abnormalities resulting from the trauma. High sodium, with fairly high urea and creatinine, suggest dehydration due to water deprivation, which seems obvious with the clinical picture. The raised creatine kinase may indicate damage to muscle cells, but the CK-MB within the normal range suggests that this is not of cardiac origin. Low glucose may be explained by temporary starvation for at least seven hours, possibly longer.

Bilirubin is quite high, and this may be due to release from damaged red blood cells, which (alongside damaged muscle cells) may partly explain the high potassium. The red cell profile is normal, but this does not preclude internal haemorrhaging. The high neutrophil count is likely to reflect the general trauma and does not imply a bacterial infection. Treatments include rehydration (which has already begun with the saline drip) with added dextrose, but also insulin (the latter to restore the hyperkalaemia) and glucose (to prevent hypoglycaemia that would probably result from the insulin), and then admission to a medical ward. Anticoagulation would need to be considered, as it is likely he is at risk of a venous thrombosis. However, the possibility of internal haemorrhage must also be considered.

Case report 11

A woman in her mid-twenties is brought to the Accident and Emergency Unit at midnight unconscious, having collapsed at a nightclub. Her friends do not consider her to be drunk but say she may well have hit her head as she fell. The subject is poorly responsive, pale and clammy, and with a high breath rate of about 25–30/minute and a Glasgow coma score of 11 (poor result 3, good result 15). Blood pressures are 110/70, pulse rate 90/minute. Serum biochemistry and blood gases are ordered.

Test	Reference range	Result	Test	Reference range	Result
Na	133–148	149	K	3.3–5.6	3.7
Urea	3.0–8.3	9.2	Creatinine	44–133	85
Glucose	<6.1	4.5	Bicarbonate	21–28	21
Bilirubin	<21	15	Alk phos	20–130	90
ALT	<41	35	Gamma GT	<45	14
Hydrogen ions (H+)	36–44	29	pH	7.36–7.44	7.47
Bicarbonate	24–32	25	PCO$_2$	4.5– 6.1	3.8
Haemoglobin	118–148	13.1	Red cell count	3.9–5.0	4.7
MCV	80–98	93.4	White cell count	4–10	5.0
Neutrophils	1.7–6.1	3.3	Lymphocytes	1.0–3.2	1.2
ESR	<10	4	Platelets	150–400	301

Interpretation

The abnormal serum results are slight hypernatraemia and uraemia, with serum bicarbonate at the bottom end of the normal range. The blood pressure is not too bad but there is somewhat of a tachycardia. The blood gas result is consistent with respiratory alkalosis (raised pH, low H$^+$ and PCO$_2$, fairly low bicarbonate), which fits in with the hyperventilation (about twice the normal rate). Note the report of possible head injury, which may have involved the brain stem.

A check of the woman's handbag found an inhaler (implying a mild lung problem), and antibiotics (implying an unknown infection). Normal glucose rules out diabetic ketoacidosis as a cause of the collapse. Electrolyte changes may be secondary to a pre-renal problem, possibly dehydration. Consider also the possibility of drug abuse causing a respiratory stimulation. The situation does not seem to be life-threatening – the respiratory rate is not extremely high, and Glasgow coma score moderate – so rest and observation may be all that is required. A saline drip may help the pre-renal uraemia.

Case report 12

This 55-year-old woman had been in intensive care for three weeks with an E Coli septicaemia being treated with ciprofloxacin. Previously acidotic and developing hypotension (SBP/DBP 110/65, despite fluid support), she was placed on warfarin and briefly on LMWH because of the risk of venous thrombembolism. However, these were cut back because of bleeding per vagina. Gross obesity (accurate BMI impossible but estimated >40) prevented many investigations. Other problems include pyrexia (38.1°C) and bilateral effusive sacral and buttock ulcers/sores. Psychologically she was anxious and depressed, refusing physiotherapy and the dietician's suggestion of a nasogastric tube. Basal crackling in both lungs was noted, with respiration shallow and forced.

Test	Reference range	Result	Test	Reference range	Result
Na	133–148	143	K	3.3–5.6	4.7
Urea	3.0–8.3	10.2	Creatinine	44–133	114
T protein	63–84	40	Albumin	35–50	23
Calcium	2.2–2.6	1.76			
Bilirubin	<21	7	Alk phos	20–130	150
ALT	<41	30	AST	<37	63
Gamma GT	<45	58	CRP	<5	37
Haemoglobin	118–148	70	Red cell count	3.9–5.0	2.5
MCV	80–98	90.1	White cell count	4–10	20.0
Neutrophils	1.7–6.1	17.9	Lymphocytes	1.0–3.2	1.5
Haematocrit	36–44	22.5	Platelets	150–400	210
Prothrombin time	11–14	19	APTT	24–34	55
Fibrinogen	1.5–4.0	2.0	ESR	<10	25

Interpretation

We already know this woman is severely ill and has numerous problems. The major haematology points are the normocytic anaemia (note bleeding per vagina, low Hct and low red cell count) and marked neutrophil leukocytosis. There is also prolonged PT (due to warfarin?) and PTT (due to what?). Fortunately she has sufficient platelets and fibrinogen to maintain haemostasis.

Major biochemistry points are uraemia (virtually to be expected), a profoundly low albumin, and low total proteins with low calcium. High CRP and ESR are to be expected in view of the septicaemia and add nothing of value. Other abnormalities are of minor clinical significance. Clinical history implies self-neglect and malnutrition, lung involvement, and the sores may be infected and/or a source of blood and fluid loss. She was about to have a four-pack blood transfusion, but died during the night.

Case report 13

A 66-year-old man of African descent self-presents to Accident and Emergency with a short (two- to three-week) history of recently developing tiredness and lethargy. He appears thin but otherwise seems well. The following blood results are obtained:

Test	Reference range	Result	Test	Reference range	Result
Na	133–148	143	K	3.3–5.6	4.3
Urea	3.0–8.3	5.0	Creatinine	44–133	92
Uric acid	<420	630	Albumin	35–50	38
Bilirubin	<21	24	Alk phos	20–130	257
ALT	<41	304	Gamma GT	<64	104
Calcium	2.2–2.6	1.97	Phosphate	0.81–1.45	1.09
CRP	<5	51			
Haemoglobin	133–167	25	Red cell count	4.3–5.7	1.85
MCV	80–98	90.6	White cell count	4–10	656
Neutrophils	1.7–6.1	71.71	Lymphocytes	1.0–3.2	13.13
Monocytes	0.2–1.0	13.13	Atypical cells	<0.02	557.9
ESR	<10	38	Platelets	150–400	30
Haematocrit	36–44	16.6	APTT	24–34	38
Prothrombin time	11–14	31			

Interpretation

With the triad of an exceptionally high WBCC, low haemoglobin and low platelets, this is clearly an acute leukaemia. High numbers of some white cell groups, reported as 71.71 and 13.13, are an artefact of the Haematology analyser. There are simply so many cells present that the machine cannot cope, so these results are incorrect. Other changes are to be expected: low red cell count and haematocrit.

However, there are other abnormalities – notably raised PT and PTT, as if the patient were on active anticoagulation, which he was not. This may reflect the extent to which the leukaemia has moved from the bone marrow to the liver. Indeed, there is clear evidence of the disease spreading, notably raised liver enzymes, and this may account for the prolonged clotting times, as the production of coagulation factors by a damaged liver would be impaired.

Remarkably, renal function seems to be unimpaired (eGFR 92ml/mim/1.73m^2). Raised CRP and ESR simply reflect very severe disease, although an infection cannot be discounted. Shortly after this report was received, the patient was due to be transferred to the leukaphoresis suite in an attempt to reduce the load of abnormal (leukaemic) cells in his blood. However, he suffered a fatal cardiac arrest whilst in transfer. The case also illustrates how rapidly this acute myeloid leukaemia developed and influenced other laboratory tests.

Case report 14

A 73-year-old diabetic female presented to Accident and Emergency with progressive shortness of breath and a two-week history of diarrhoea. Her medications included aspirin, and blood pressure lowering drugs irbesartan and hydrochlorothiazide, and metformin. On examination, she was oliguric, disorientated and confused, with a respiratory rate of 32 breaths/minute, systolic/diastolic blood pressures of 76/44mmHg, and a pulse rate 125 beats/minute. Bloods were as follows:

Test	Reference range	Result	Test	Reference range	Result
Haemoglobin	118–148	129	White cell count	4.0–10.0	7.0
Red cell count	4.3–5.7	4.7	MCV	80–98	85.5
Platelets	140–400	216	ESR	<10	12
HbA1c	3.8–6.2	9.1*	HbA1c	48–58**	80***
Neutrophils	2.0–7.0	4.5	Lymphocytes	1.0–3.0	1.8

Na	133–144	133	K	3.4–5.1	6.3
Urea	3.0–8.3	19.5	Creatinine	44–144	279
eGFR	>90	15.3	Albumin	35–50	39

Bilirubin	<21	8	Alk phos	20–130	47
AST	10–50	39	ALT	5–42	29
Gamma GT	10–50	39	Lactate	0.7–1.0	17.4
CRP	<5	<5	Glucose	3.3–5.5	9.p

pH	7.35–7.45	6.72	PCO_2	4.7–6.0	1.87
PO_2	12.0–14.6	14.1	Bicarbonate	24– 29	12

HbA1c results: *%

**Reference range for known diabetics

***mmol/mol

Interpretation

The haematology shows a minimally increased ESR, but a markedly abnormal HbA1c, implying months of hyperglycaemia. As for the biochemistry, there is hyperkalaemia, raised urea and creatinine, the latter giving a low eGFR, synonymous with Stage IV chronic kidney disease. LFTs are normal, but there is markedly raised lactate and hyperglycaemia. All blood gas indices are low, except the oxygen partial pressure.

The picture is of clear diabetic lactic acidosis. It may possibly also be described as diabetic ketoacidosis, but ketones have not been directly measured. Precipitating factors include the diarrhoea, predisposing to dehydration (hence the low blood pressure), leading to the impaired perfusion of organs. The normal white cell count and CRP rule out septicaemia, which commonly causes an acidosis. Indeed, factors precipitating this condition include infections, which are clearly not present in this case.

Urgent treatment is demanded, and is likely to be led by the need to vigorously rehydrate, probably with intravenous fluids, but also bicarbonate supplements to reverse the acidosis. This may also help the hyperkalaemia. An additional treatment is likely to be insulin, but if so, there must be sufficient plasma glucose. The borderline low sodium may be due to the osmotic diuresis caused by the hyperglycaemia. Once stable, a complete overhaul of the patient's care is required.

Part 4

Appendices

Appendix 1:
Special situations (pregnancy, the neonate, and the elderly)

Appendix 1 brings together three separate areas that, individually, would not normally warrant too much attention in the 'routine' sense. There are changes in blood results that arise in pregnancy, in early life, and in late life, so a combined approach will be taken. However, it must be stressed that clinical decisions in these situations demand a high level of experience and interpretation.

Key words and pathological expressions:

Anaemia
Factor Xa
Gestational diabetes
Pre-eclampsia
Haemoglobinopathy
Neonatal jaundice
Neonatal screening
Venothromboembolism

Pregnancy

It is little surprise that there are numerous changes to a woman's blood whilst she is carrying a child. However, these are entirely physiological: indeed, pregnancy is an indication of good overall health – the pregnant woman should not automatically be viewed as a patient. Reference ranges in pregnancy can be found in Appendix 3 (see page 144).

Anaemia

This is perhaps one of the best-known haematology features of pregnancy, and is probably due to a number of factors, such as increased plasma volume. Plasma volume increases by up to 40% (but with wide individual variations) during the first two trimesters, whereas the red cell mass increases by perhaps only 25%. The consequences are often a fall in haemoglobin (e.g. to 100–110 g/L) in weeks 16 to 40. An additional explanation for anaemia is the increased demand for iron by the foetus.

The healthy female of reproductive age needs about 2–3 milligrams of iron daily, but when pregnant this rises to 3–4 milligrams. She will therefore be at risk of an iron-deficient anaemia without a change in diet. In the immediate post-partum period, blood lost during labour needs to be replaced and so extra iron will be needed. There is also an extra need for micronutrients such as vitamin B_{12} and folate, and supplements may be needed to reduce the risk of certain anaemias and of neural tube defects in the infant. Red cells can also increase their size, as is assessed by the mean cell volume (MCV), often by 5 to 10fL.

Thrombosis

Anticoagulation must be considered even before a woman becomes pregnant, as warfarin can cross the placenta to produce foetal abnormalities, and is therefore contraindicated. If a woman on warfarin (regardless of the reason, such as for antiphospholipid syndrome, deep vein thrombosis [DVT] or pulmonary embolism [PE], as introduced in Chapter 3) is considering pregnancy, she needs to come off warfarin and use LMWH. Monitoring of the latter, if necessary, would be by the blood test for coagulation Factor Xa.

Pregnancy in itself brings a risk of DVT and/or PE, but this risk is generally so small that anticoagulation with a LMWH is not called for. However, if a woman does have a DVT whilst pregnant, she will probably need to go onto a LMWH, the activity of which will need to be monitored by levels of Factor Xa. The reasons for this increased risk of venothromboembolism (VTE) are unclear but may be related to increased levels of clotting factors such as prothrombin, Factor VIII and fibrinogen.

There may also be a reduced ability to remove a clot once it has formed (this is called fibrinolysis). For those who have had a single VTE, even with a family history of thrombophilia, the initial dose should be five days of a higher weight-adjusted LMWH (preferably in two divided doses), followed by a prophylactic dose for the rest of the pregnancy. This will need to be continued post-partum with at least six weeks of either warfarin or LMWH, although some women may need anticoagulation for up to six months.

Once the baby has been delivered, the woman is even more at risk of DVT or PE. Popular reasons why this entirely healthy condition confers such a risk of thrombosis include a reduction in the risk of post-partum haemorrhage, or possibly that the growing uterus slows venous blood return up the inferior vena cava in the lower abdomen. The risk of DVT in the six weeks post partum is three times the ante-partum risk, whilst the risk of PE is eight times higher. Diagnosis of VTE is made more difficult by the fact that pregnancy alone can confer raised D-dimers, so non-invasive methods (such as ultrasound) are required. Post-partum, warfarin can be used, and DVT can be managed as for non-pregnant women, but not with unfractionated heparin as LMWH safety data is better. The Royal College of Obstetrics and Gynaecology (www.rcog.org.uk) have their own guidelines for managing risk of VTE.

Perhaps 8 to 10% of women will experience a fall in their platelet count during pregnancy, and this may be to below the normal range (i.e. a thrombocytopenia). However, this is rarely associated with a risk of significant bleeding.

Apart from DVT and PE, pregnant women are at risk of a very rare type of haemolytic anaemia, which manifests with elevated liver enzymes (for LFTs, see Chapter 8, page 76) and low platelets. (H for haemolysis, EL for elevated liver enzymes, and LP for low platelet count together give the acronym HELLP.) Another dangerous condition is a generalised coagulopathy called disseminated intravascular coagulation (DIC), which may require admission to an intensive care unit. If DIC and HELLP co-exist, the induction of labour or a caesarean section may be indicated.

Biochemistry

The numerous physiological changes during pregnancy mean that many indices applicable in non-pregnant woman are simply not valid (see Appendix 3, page 142). The weight gain of perhaps 12 kilograms includes about 5 litres of water, perhaps a litre of which contributes (as in haematology) to a haemodilution. In consequence, the glomerular filtration rate rises, so urea and creatinine levels are lower.

Diabetes, if present before pregnancy or developing during pregnancy (i.e. gestational diabetes), is associated with fetal mortality and morbidity (such as high birth weight and respiratory distress). Thus, adequate control of hyperglycaemia is required, although excess glucose in the urine (i.e. glycosuria) is common because of changes in renal function and does not necessarily imply a glycaemic pathology.

One of the more common and serious complications of pregnancy, pre-eclampsia, is characterised early on by hypertension and later by ankle oedema. The laboratory can generally demonstrate increasing serum urate, and later rising serum urea and creatinine (i.e. the reverse of a healthy pregnancy), resulting from a falling glomerular filtration rate. A further consequence is proteinuria – generally detected by a urine dipstick. If untreated, pre-eclampsia leads to life-threatening eclampsia.

Prolactin is known to be higher in women than men (103–497mU/L and 86–324mU/L respectively), with levels up to 8,000 in pregnancy. Similarly, oestrogen, progesterone, testosterone, luteinising hormone and follicle stimulating hormone all vary between the sexes, and in women depend on their age and the phase of their menstrual cycle.

Immunology and blood transfusion

Many laboratories offer ante-natal testing for antibodies to a number of pathogens that include hepatitis B (surface antigen and its antibody), HIV, syphilis and rubella. Antenatal screening for Rh D will identify those D negative women who are likely to need anti-D immunoglobulin prophylaxis to reduce the risk of future haemolytic disease of the newborn (HDN). At a later stage, it is possible to determine if this has been successful by testing for anti-D antibodies. Other antibodies that can be tested for include the K antigen and the C antigen.

Paediatrics

It is hardly surprising that the transition from intra-uterine to independent life demands numerous changes, and there are therefore differences in a child's blood compared to that of adolescents and adults. Once more, these differences are entirely physiological. A crucial aspect of paediatric blood science is the need to refer to local reference ranges and guidelines. Notably, such values in textbooks often demonstrate considerable variation. A second caveat is the variation in the definition (days, weeks, months and years of life) of neonate, infant, child and even adolescent. Some normal/reference values are provided in Appendix 3 (see pages 145–7).

Haematology

The haemoglobin, red cell count and mean cell volume vary considerably and change rapidly in the first three months of independent life, and the transition to 'adult' levels of many blood indices may take additional months and even years. Indeed, haemoglobin levels at birth may be regarded in adult terms as polycythaemia (e.g. 160–190g/L in the neonate, compared to perhaps 125–170g/L in the adult), rise a little more in the 24 hours that follow, and then fall. By six months, levels are around the lower limit of normal for an adult (maybe 125g/L). Consequently, the definition of anaemia should not be made according to adult values. Causes of anaemia, if present, include haemolytic disease of the newborn, infections and haemoglobinopathy (the latter largely sickle cell disease and thalassaemia). Notably, perhaps 30% of all new cases of haemoglobinopathy could not be predicted by the genetic status of the parents and would thus be due to unforeseen mutation.

Prematurity brings its own special problems, one of which may be an anaemia due to nutritional deficiencies such as iron and vitamin B_{12}. Insufficient vitamin K may lead to disorders of haemostasis, with bruising and bleeding, as certain coagulation proteins are reliant on this micronutrient. Healthy infants have 'adult' levels of platelets, but neonatal thrombocytopenia is present in up to a quarter of babies referred to neonate intensive care units.

Biochemistry

The kidney should be fully formed and operational by week 36 of gestation, although the glomerular filtration rate is relatively low at birth. Thus serum creatinine rises in the immediate neonatal period, falls after about four weeks and then remains low for perhaps five years, when levels rise to those of adults.

The liver is a relatively late-developing organ. In the first few weeks of life it may not be capable of metabolising all its own bilirubin (previously managed by the mother), which could result in jaundice. This should resolve rapidly as the liver matures. However, jaundice in the first 24 hours is almost all pathological. More concerning reasons for jaundice include haemolytic disease of the newborn or abnormalities of the liver. It follows that the premature child will be at risk of additional metabolic problems.

Levels of oestrogen, progesterone, testosterone, luteinising hormone and follicle stimulating hormone are all low or absent before puberty. Indeed, increased levels of these hormones, possibly arising from a gonadal malignancy before this stage, nevertheless often define precocious puberty.

Neonatal screening

Several pathological conditions are apparent within the first year of birth and can be screened for in the first few days of life, often using a spot of blood obtained about a week about birth. Perhaps the best-known biochemistry examples of this are for congenital hypothyroidism and phenylketonuria (PKU). The former (present in 1/3,500 live births in the UK), if untreated, can result in irreversible cretinism – the most common cause being failure of the thyroid gland to develop adequately and produce the thyroid hormones T3 and thyroxine (see Chapter 11, page 99). This deficiency, once detected, results in raised TSH – the basis of the relevant blood test and so the diagnosis. If discovered, treatment is with small doses of thyroxine that can be increased to an adult dose as the child approaches its teenage years.

PKU (present in 1 in 10,000 live births in the UK) is the result of an error in amino-acid metabolism (lack of a particular enzyme). The clinical consequences of this include neonatal irritability, poor feeding, eczema and fair hair with blue eyes. The later consequence of mental retardation can be minimised with a diet low in the amino acid phenylalanine.

In paediatrics, a positive or equivocal result should always be confirmed by a repeat test.

The elderly

The aging process is inevitable and is associated with many changes as physiology merges with pathology. Abnormal laboratory results are more common in the aged because they have more disease, and the increased use of prescription drugs is likely to cloud a diagnosis. There are relatively few instances where the reference range varies with age in the absence of clear disease. These include:

- Renal function, manifesting as a deterioration in the GFR with age: Indeed, both common calculators input age into their equations.
- Sex hormones: Decreasing fertility in both sexes is associated with reduced levels of sex hormones, and is marked in women around the age of 50.
- Levels of growth hormones peak in the teenage years and fall markedly and progressively after the age of 20.
- Some accept that ESR rises 'normally' with age, although others contend that this reflects a low level of pathology.
- Similarly, others are prepared to accept a lower level of haemoglobin in the elderly that would stimulate an investigation in someone a decade younger.
- Age-related increase in the reference range for prostate specific antigen: Age 50–59 <3; age 60–69 <4; age 70+ <5.

Appendix 2:
Physiotherapy and podiatry

Changes in the NHS have brought about the opportunity for practitioners in these two professions to take a leading role in the diagnosis and management of their patients. This is likely to develop further, as physiotherapists and podiatrists develop the same prescriber status as many nurses. Blood tests can help in both these processes.

Physiotherapy

There are several separate areas of the body and its diseases to consider.

Musculoskeletal disease

In seeking to clarify a diagnosis of leg, hip and back pain, tests of inflammation may be useful in order to differentiate osteo- and rheumatoid arthritis (RA). The former is unlikely to have abnormal inflammatory markers (ESR, CRP, white cell count), whereas these are common in the latter. A raised rheumatoid factor (RF) leads to a strong suspicion of RA, but joint disease and clinical history are also important. The diagnostic criteria for RA include factors such as prolonged early morning stiffness and palindromic joint pain and swelling.

RF is also often raised in systemic lupus erythematosus, but an abnormal level of anti-nuclear antibodies are common, as are autoantibodies to DNA. Other diseases in this area include polymyalgia rheumatica (PMR – literally rheumatic pain of many muscles) and temporal arteritis, but neither of these have precise tests. However, as with all such diseases, increased ESR and CRP can be expected.

Ankylosing spondylitis (AS) lacks a definitive blood test, as the disease is generally restricted to the lower vertebrae and pelvis. Many patients are positive for HLA-B27, although this has a particularly poor sensitivity and specificity (that is, many people with this HLA type do not have AS, and many AS patients are negative for B27). Do not expect abnormalities in bone markers such as calcium, and increased systemic markers of inflammation are unlikely. Muscle-wasting diseases, such as polymyositis, may be associated with increased creatine kinase.

Bone and orthopaedics

Lack of vitamin D is the cause of osteomalacia (rickets in children), whilst Paget's disease (associated with bone pain and deformity) is often linked with a raised alkaline phosphatase. Gout (acute pain in joints, often accompanied by swelling) is caused by deposits of crystals of uric acid/urate in the tissues and joints. These are in turn the result of increased levels of plasma uric acid/urate, the most common causes of which are (in order) excess alcohol (>42 units/week), use of diuretic drugs, renal impairment and obesity (BMI >30).

Gout can be differentiated from pseudogout, as a common form of the latter is due to the deposition of calcium pyrophosphate crystals, and so is also known as chondrocalcinosis and pyrophosphate arthropathy. This requires a biopsy or sample of the synovial fluid to be sent to the laboratory.

Bone pain may be due to myeloma and secondary deposits of cancer (such as of the prostate and breast). In such cases, increased bone markers (calcium, alkaline phosphatase) may be helpful. There are no markers of breast cancer, but in prostate cancer levels of prostate specific antigen (PSA) are often increased. Physiotherapy after surgery, especially orthopaedic, may need to take account of anticoagulation.

Stroke

There are no tests for this condition, or its precursor of transient ischaemic attack (TIA). However, both TIA and stroke may have been precipitated by any combination of abnormal lipids (increased total and low density lipoprotein cholesterol and triglycerides, with low high density lipoprotein cholesterol), high blood pressure, diabetes (calling for HbA1c) and/or atrial fibrillation (diagnosed by ECG).

The chest/respiratory

Pains in the chest are symptoms of both coronary artery disease (where the risk factor for stroke and TIA are also relevant in angina) and pulmonary embolism, and both of these should be addressed urgently in Accident and Emergency. Relevant blood tests are creatine kinase, CK-MB and troponins. If pulmonary embolism is suspected, it may be excluded by normal levels of D-dimers.

There are no specific blood tests in chronic obstructive pulmonary disease, though non-specific markers of inflammation may be raised. In severe and acute asthma there may be raised IgE, but pulmonary function tests are probably more important.

For details of the classification of rheumatic diseases, see the website of the American college of Rheumatology at:

**www.rheumatology.org/practice/clinical/classification/classification_criteria_for_
rheumatic_diseases**

Podiatry

Although podiatrists are principally interested in the leg below the knee, disease of the foot may have systemic manifestations. Perhaps the leading blood tests in podiatry are for diabetes, which are fasting plasma glucose, the OGTT and HbA1c (as discussed extensively in Chapter 9, see page 86). The primary consequence of this disease is peripheral artery disease, with loss of pedal pulses, digital hypoxia and eventual gangrene. Blood tests are effective in supporting the diagnosis and the practitioner may consider recommending the use of, or more aggressive management of, lipid-lowering and blood-pressure lowering agents in addition to hypoglycaemics.

Those podiatrists about to undertake debridement, nail work and other surgery must be aware of the use of anticoagulants such as warfarin, and a consequent risk of excessive bleeding (see Chapter 3, page 35). Use of aspirin or NSAIDs is less of an issue.

Suspected bacterial infections, perhaps of venous ulcers, may call for measurement of the white blood cell counts, ESR and CRP as markers of inflammation. Topical application of antibiotics may be appropriate. There are no blood tests for fungal infections.

Other diseases of relevance for podiatrists include:

- Osteomalacia/rickets: Caused by lack of vitamin D, although diagnosis cannot be made without an X-ray.
- Osteomyelitis: There are no truly valuable blood tests, although general tests of inflammation (ESR/white cell count/CRP) may be helpful. This condition is generally diagnosed clinically and by X-ray of the foot, where there is likely to be evidence of bone destruction.
- Paget's disease: Alkaline phosphatase is essential and X-ray may be used to define abnormal bone structure.
- The bone aspects of renal osteodystrophy often affect the legs and foot, and if suspected the appropriate tests are urea and electrolytes (which are likely to be increased) and calcium (which is likely to be low).
- Rheumatoid arthritis/osteoarthritis: As above, general tests of inflammation, but also rheumatoid factor (see Chapters 5 and 9).
- Muscle-wasting diseases, such as polymyositis, may be associated with increased creatine kinase.
- Gout in a painful and swollen toe may be confirmed with levels of uric acid, and also U&Es.

Notably, many of these are also relevant to physiotherapists.

Appendix 3:
Adult reference ranges

Adult reference ranges for common blood results

NB: These ranges may differ from those used in your own hospital; remember, you must practise according to your local laboratory.

Analyte	Reference range	Units
Alanine aminotransferase	5–42	IU/L
Albumin	35–50	g/L
Alkaline phosphatase	20–120	IU/L
Amylase	<300	IU/L
Aspartate aminotransferase	10–50	IU/L
Basophils	0.02–1.0	10^9/L
Bicarbonate (hydrogen carbonate)	24–29	mmol/L
Bilirubin	<21	μmol/L
Blast/atypical cells	<0.02	10^9/L
Calcium	2.2–2.6	mmol/L
Total cholesterol	<5.0	mmol/L
Low density lipoprotein cholesterol	<3.0	mmol/L
High density lipoprotein cholesterol	>1.2	mmol/L
C-reactive protein	<10	mg/L
Creatinine	71–133	μmol/L
D-dimers*	<500	Units/mL
eGFR	>90	ml/min/1.73m^2
Eosinophils	0.02–0.5	10^9/L
Erythrocyte sedimentation rate	<10	mm/hour
Fibrinogen	1.5–4.0	g/L
Gamma-glutamyl transferase	5–55	IU/L
Glucose (fasting)	3.5–5.5	mmol/L

Haematocrit (female)	0.33–0.47	L/L
Haematocrit (male)	0.35–0.53	L/L
Haemoglobin (female)	118–148	g/L
Haemoglobin (male)	133–167	g/L
International normalised ratio	2–3 or 3–4	
Lactate	0.7–1.9	mmol/L
Lactate dehydrogenase	240–480	IU/L
Lymphocytes	1.0–3.0	10^9/L
Magnesium	0.8–1.2	mmol/L
Mean cell haemoglobin	26–33	pg
Mean cell haemoglobin concentration	330–370	pg/L
Mean cell volume	77–98	fL
Monocytes	0.2–1.0	10^9/L
Neutrophils	2.0–7.0	10^9/L
Parathyroid hormone	1–6	pmol/L
Partial thromboplastin time	24–34	seconds
PCO_2	4.7–6.0	kPa
PO_2	12–14.6	kPa
pH	7.35–7.45	$-\log_{10}[H^+]$
Phosphate	0.8–1.4	mmol/L
Plasma viscosity (at 25° C)	1.5–1.72	mPa/s
Platelets	143–400	10^9/L
Potassium	3.8–5.0	mmol/L
Protein	60–80	g/L
Prothrombin time	11–14	seconds
PSA (prostate specific antigen)**	<3 to <5	ng/mL
Red blood cell count (female)	3.9–5.0	10^{12}/L
Red blood cell count (male)	4.3–5.7	10^{12}/L
Sodium	135–145	mmol/L
Thyroid stimulating hormone	0.2–3.5	mU/L
Triglycerides	<1.7	mmol/L

Urate/uric acid		0.1–0.42	mmol/L
Urea		3.3–6.7	mmol/L
White blood cells		4.0–10.0	10^9/L

* Dependent on method

** Age dependent

Selected biochemistry and haematology normal/reference values in pregnancy

Analyte	Unit	Non-pregnant normal range	Pregnant normal range
Alanine aminotransferase	IU/L	<50	<30
Albumin	g/L	40–52	32–42
Alkaline phosphatase	IU/L	80–280	175–400
Aspartate aminotransferase	IU/L	<60	<31
Bicarbonate	mmol/L	21–28	18–28
Bilirubin	μmol/L	<21	<14
Blood H^+	nmol/L	35–45	34–42
Blood PCO_2	kPa	4.4–5.6	3.0-5.0
Calcium	mmol/L	2.2–2.6	2.2–2.8
Daily iron requirement	mg	2–3	3–4
ESR	mm/hour	<10	30–100
Fasting glucose	mmol/L	<6	<5
Fibrinogen	g/L	1.5–3.5	2.5–4.5
Haematocrit	Proportion	0.33–0.47	0.31–0.45
Haemoglobin	g/L	118–148	100–140
MCV	fL	77–100	81–103
Potassium	mmol/L	3.4–5.1	3.2–4.6
Sodium	mmol/L	133–144	131–140

Total protein	g/L		63–84	53–74
Urea	mmol/L		3.0–8.3	1.0–3.8
White blood cell count	109/L		3.5–11	6–14

Remember that many indices vary between the sexes even in the absence of pregnancy. As with other 'normal/reference ranges', the above list is provided for perspective and should NOT be used in your own clinical setting, where your local normal/reference ranges will apply. Present data pooled from textbooks by Hacker et al., Drife et al., and others (see Recommended textbooks, page 148).

Selected biochemistry normal /reference values in neonatalogy and paediatrics

Analyte	Unit		Neonatal/ infant/child normal range	Adult normal range
Albumin	g/L	Neonate	25–45	35–60
		1–3 months	30–42	
		Child	35–55	
Alkaline Phosphatase	IU/L	Neonate	60–240	20–130
		1 month–1 year	52–444	
		2–9 years	60–310	
		Pubertal	60–400	
Amylase	IU/L	Neonate	<50	<110
		1–3 months	<100	
		Up to 1st year	<130	
Bilirubin	μmol/L	1st day	<65	<21
		2nd day	<115	
		3rd–5th day	<155	
		Up to 1st month	<17	
Calcium	mmol/L	24–48 hours	1.8–3.0	2.2–2.6
		Up to 1st week	2.2–2.7	

Creatine kinase (total)	IU/L	Neonate 1 month 1 year	<600 <400 <300	<150
Creatinine	μmol/L	Up to 2 weeks 2–4 weeks 1 month–3 years 4–6 years 7–9 years 10–12 years 13–15 years 16–18 years	<100 <55 <40 <46 10–56 30–60 40–80 40–96	44–133
Gamma GT	IU/L	Neonate 1 month–1 year Over 1 year	<200 <150 <30	<70
Glucose	mmol/L	1st day After 1st day Up to 1st month	2.2–3.3 2.6–5.5 3.6–5.4	3.0–6.0
Potassium	mmol/L	Up to 2 weeks 2 weeks–3 months Over 3 months	3.5–6.0 3.3–5.0 3.5–5.0	3.4–5.1
Total protein	g/L	Neonate Infant Child	52–70 59–70 60–80	63–84
Urea	mmol/L	1 month Up to 1st year Years 1–7 Over 7 years	2.0–5.0 2.5–6.0 3.5–6.5 2.5– 6.5	3.0–8.3

Selected haematology normal/reference values in neonatalogy and paediatrics

Age	Hb (g/L)	MCV fL	WBCC x 109/L
Birth	149–237	100–130	6–26
2 weeks	134–205	95–120	6–21
1 month	110–180	90–105	5–20
2 months	94–130	84–95	5–18
1 year	113–141	73–88	6–17
2–6 years	101–138	73–88	6–17
6–12 years	111–147	77–91	4.5–14.5
12–18 years			
Male	121–166	78–95	4.5–13
Female	121–151	78–95	4.5–13

As with other 'normal/reference ranges', the above list is provided for perspective and should NOT be used in your own clinical setting, where your local normal/reference ranges will apply. For example, definitions of neonate, infant and child vary markedly. Present data pooled from textbooks by O'Callaghan & Stephenson, Lissauer & Clayden, and others (see below).

Recommended textbooks

Drife, J. & Magowan, B. (2004). *Clinical Obstetrics and Gynaecology.* Philadelphia, USA: Elsevier, Saunders.

Hacker, N.F., Moore, J.G. & Gambone, J.C. (2004). *Essentials of Obstetrics and Gynaecology.* Philadelphia, USA: Elsevier, Saunders.

Lissauer, T. & Clayden, G. (2001). *Illustrated Textbook of Paediatrics.* Philadelphia, USA: Elsevier, Mosby.

O'Callaghan, C. & Stephenson, T. (2004). *Pocket Paediatrics.* Philadelphia, USA: Elsevier, Churchill Livingstone.

Futher reading

I am happy to recommend the following textbooks. They all provide considerably more information than this short work.

Biomedical Sciences: Essential Laboratory Medicine
R.K. Iles & S.M. Doherty (eds), Wiley Blackwell, Chichester, 2012

Clinical Biochemistry
N. Ahmed (ed.), Oxford University Press, Oxford, 2011

Clinical Biochemistry: An illustrated Colour Text
A. Gaw, R.A. Cowan, D.J. O'Reilly, M.J. Stewart & J. Shepherd, Mosby, London, 2004

Haematology
G. Moore, G. Knight & A. Blann. Oxford University Press, Oxford, 2011

Immunology
A. Hall & C. Yates (eds), Oxford University Press, Oxford, 2010

Medicinal Biochemistry at a Glance (3rd edn)
J.G. Salway, Wiley Blackwell, Chichester UK, 2012

Roitt's Essential Immunology (12th edn)
P.L. Delves, S.J. Martin, D.R. Burton & I.M. Roitt , Wiley Blackwell, Chichester, 2011

Transfusion and Transplantation Science
R. Knight (ed.), Oxford University Press, Oxford, 2013

Transfusion Medicine (3rd edn)
J. McCullough, Wiley Blackwell, Chichester, 2012

Index